Jeffrey D. Hamilton, DMin

Gestalt in Pastoral Care and Counseling
A Holistic Approach

Pre-publication
REVIEWS,
COMMENTARIES,
EVALUATIONS . . .

"**J**effrey Hamilton's exploration of Gestalt is well-timed for a generation of seminarians and clergy that has not been exposed to this powerful therapeutic tool. The strength of his book rests in its accessible language, clear illustrations of somewhat unfamiliar terminology, and the relevance of Gestalt for the vocational demands of pastoral caring and leadership. His compassion and competence as a pastor and therapist are also quite evident."

Frank J. Stalfa, Jr., DMin
Professor of Pastoral Theology,
Lancaster Theological Seminary

"**D**r. Hamilton has given us a summary of basic concepts of Gestalt in a very readable question and answer format that is simple, but never simplistic. Its concepts are very useful and helpful to pastors in church administration as well as in more traditional pastoral care and counseling. It is an interesting review for those familiar with Gestalt, and for those not familiar, a motivation to further learn its theory, and especially its practice, as well as being practical in and of itself. I highly recommend it."

Sue Webb Cardwell, PhD
Professor Emerita of Psychology
and Counseling and Psychologist,
Christian Theological Seminary;
Past President, AAPC

Gestalt in Pastoral Care and Counseling
A Holistic Approach

Gestalt in Pastoral Care and Counseling
A Holistic Approach

Jeffrey D. Hamilton, DMin

Published by

The Haworth Pastoral Press, an imprint of The Haworth Press, Inc., 10 Alice Street, Binghamton, NY 13904-1580

Cover design by Marylouise E. Doyle.

Library of Congress Cataloging-in-Publication Data

Hamilton, Jeffrey D.
    Gestalt in pastoral care and counseling : a holistic approach / Jeffrey D. Hamilton.
      p.   cm.
    Includes bibliographical references and index.
    ISBN 0-7890-0238-8 (alk. paper)
     1. Pastoral counseling. 2. Gestalt psychology. I. Title.
BV4012.2.H34 1997
253'.5-dc21

ISBN 0-7890-0148-9 (alk. paper)   96-52302
                                                      CIP

In memory of two persons:
William J. Hamilton, my father
and
Tim LeBar, PhD, mentor and guide

And in thanks to:
Marsha Fields-Jones, MSSA,
Who believed in the project before it was born
and
Howard H. Fink, PhD, who taught me the value of living
in the here and now in my life and my work

ABOUT THE AUTHOR

Jeffrey D. Hamilton, DMin, is an ordained minister in the United Church of Christ and a Pastoral Counselor at Miami Valley Hospital in Dayton, Ohio. He completed his post-graduate training at the Gestalt Institute of Cleveland and the Dayton Institute for Marriage and Family Therapy. After serving local congregations in Central Pennsylvania, he completed his residency in Clinical Pastoral Education at Abington Memorial Hospital. He began his career in pastoral ministry at Miami Valley Hospital as chaplain in the Critical Care and Trauma Departments, joining the pastoral counseling staff in 1986. Reverend Hamilton is a member of the American Association of Pastoral Counselors and a Certified Chaplain and Fellow of the College of Chaplains. He teaches widely in the areas of lay pastoral ministry, ministry to persons living with AIDS, and small group development. He received his DMin from United Theological Seminary in Dayton, Ohio; his MDiv from Lancaster Theological Seminary in Lancaster, Pennsylvania; and his MSSA from Case Western Reserve in Cleveland, Ohio.

CONTENTS

Foreword

Gestalt theorists and therapists are not known for their prolific writing. They practice. All the more valuable, then, are works that convey how religious professionals–clergy, pastoral counselors, and chaplains–can utilize the insights of Gestalt therapy in their religion-friendly practice.

Jeffrey Hamilton has created a resource that conveys the theory of Gestalt in bite-sized, easy-to-understand, question/answer format. The caregiver need not identify with this school of psychotherapy to benefit from this material, for digesting it helps the caregiver to be more fully present, to attend to boundaries, to be more vitally observant–traits that are used in all schools of therapy.

A long way from Fritz Perls' emphasis upon self-support, divorced from dependency upon God, Hamilton's work unabashedly integrates theology and biblical stories within the therapeutic process. It is not surprising that the theology most cited by Hamilton is "process theology" and that the hope that is claimed in the telling of the individuals' stories is a "relational hope."

Object Relations therapy and approaches to family therapy have dominated continuing education opportunities for clergy in the past decade. Yet Gestalt therapy, with its analysis of the cycle of experience, emphasis on attention, ability to prod us to see the obvious, and clever work with resistance, is not only a marvelous tool for the counselor, but also for the preacher and leader of Bible Study.

Three case studies are presented in the last section: work with an individual, a couple, and a group. Although brief descriptions, these give clues to how the reader can wisely implement the theory and practice.

Carolyn Stahl Bohler
Emma Sanborn Tousant Professor
Pastoral Theology and Counseling
United Theological Seminary
Dayton, Ohio

Acknowledgments

I want to acknowledge the many people who supported, taught, and coerced me during this project's journey.

I want to thank my wife Robin for her patience as this project took shape.

Thanks to my friends for encouraging me when the work got difficult. I thank the Department of Pastoral Care and Counseling of Miami Valley Hospital in Dayton, Ohio, for their prayers, support, and time.

I also thank Robert Webber, PhD, of Lancaster Theological Seminary, who showed me that the Scriptures can be a living model for pastoral care.

Without the faculty, staff, and fellow students of The Gestalt Institute of Cleveland, none of this could have happened. There are too many people in this "home away from home" to mention, but a few need to be recognized for directing my three years of training there: Frances Baker, John Carter, Rainette E. Franz, Veronica Harper, Francis Harris, Dan Jones, Tim LeBar, Dorothy Simonovich, Jody Niinita Telfair, and Les Wyman. I am also grateful to a number of faculty members who helped shape my view of myself and my ministry: Jay Brinegar, Mwalimu Imara, and Tyson Merrill.

Dr. Carolyn Bohler and the students of United Theological Seminary are due thanks for backing and trying out my idea.

I am grateful to The Haworth Press for giving me an answer I did not expect.

Finally, thanks to the Holy Spirit who brought this whole idea to fruition.

Introduction

A QUESTION OF LANGUAGE: TO WHOM IS THIS TEXT AIMED, AND WHAT DO WE CALL THEM?

This text is aimed at ministers. So, what term do I use to speak of these men and women? What do ministers call themselves? Some are pastors; some are counselors; others are educators, chaplains, administrators, missionaries, lay ministers, and more. The question is, "What do we call these people in these people?" I am indebted to Gordon E. Jackson for prompting me to ask the question and for supplying the answer.

He shares, to paraphrase, that to use the term "counselor" seems limiting and formal. Indeed, pastoral counseling is only one part of ministry. "Therapist" is too foreign. He states,

> Finally, I decided on the word, carer, partially because of its history in the Christian community, and partially because of the emotional richness that seems to inhere in the term for many people.[1]

As a matter of form throughout the text, I will use the terms "carer" or "pastoral carer" to identify people engaged in ministry. These can include those engaged in any aspect or form of ministry.

Inclusive language is a priority in this text. Alterations in text from the authors original word choice will be marked by brackets.

AN INTRODUCTION TO THE MODEL IN MINISTRY

The material that follows is the core curriculum from the course "Principles of Gestalt Theory" as presented at United Theological

1

Seminary as an implementation of my Doctor of Ministry Project. Throughout this text, cases are presented to illustrate specific concepts. These, as well as the case studies, were presented as "thread cases" throughout the class in an effort to illustrate the principles of Gestalt theory in action. In addition, students brought in material of their own to be discussed in class.

The section "The Gestalt Cycle of Experience" poses a challenge with regard to whom to credit for concepts and techniques, most especially regarding the "undoing" of resistances. The ideas and techniques presented were gleaned from conversations and lectures by Gestalt Institute of Cleveland faculty and students.

The style of the project was borrowed from *Scharff Notes: A Primer of Object Relations Therapy.*[2] I found the style helpful in my own learning and thought it would be useful to others. The actual questions consist primarily of those asked by the students in the project class, as well as my fellow students at the Gestalt Institute of Cleveland.

The model was also shaped by the context of my ministry. I serve as a staff member in a hospital-based pastoral counseling center. As a department, we include chaplains, CPE students and supervisors, as well as the pastoral counseling staff. Many of the examples of ministry in the project come from the collaborative nature of our department and our work.

Gestalt was chosen as a theory to be explored for several reasons. First, my personal exposure to it had consistently felt affirming of my life and faith. As I began my formal studies, I imagined the natural use of the cycle of experience by pastoral care providers. Finally, I had the good fortune of working with a master Gestalt therapist. Through his support, I began to claim Gestalt as my own, and a theory to be shared.

WHAT IS GESTALT AND HOW DOES IT APPLY TO PASTORAL CARING?

When I ask people what comes to mind when I mention "Gestalt," I hear: "empty chair," "hitting pillows," and "dream work." People speak of the techniques attributed to Gestalt practice, not the highly developed theory that surrounds them. Gestalt is much more than technique and terminology.

Gestalt . . . is more than an effective psychotherapy; it is a way of seeing and knowing, an action approach that emphasizes dynamic awareness rather than introspection.[3]

> The method of Gestalt therapy is phenomenological and dialogic, focusing upon bringing immediate and present experience into greater clarity and increasing awareness. Explanations and interpretations are considered less reliable than what is directly perceived and felt. Gestalt therapy treats with equal respect the immediate experience of both patient and therapist.[4]

Gestalt theory is a "here and now" theory. Its goal is to aid the individuals, carers, and those receiving the care to be more aware of the moment. Both parties are alive *in the moment* to what occurs between them and within themselves. The wholeness of the relationship is understood as valuable. Too often, it seems, pastoral carers are taught ways of acting, ways of behaving. They are taught how to be "active listeners" and to pose questions to aid in understanding. In essence, they are taught to have a clear boundary between themselves and the other person. Often, they are told not to reveal the impact of a statement on themselves to the recipient of their care.

I recall reviewing a pastoral call with my supervising pastor during my first field placement while in seminary. All seemed to be going well until I mentioned, "I told her (the church member) that I felt sad as she told me the story." His response was immediate, "It doesn't matter what you felt. She does not need to know it. You're there for her, and not for you." Even then, I was bothered by the idea that to behave as a professional I needed to deny sharing with another what had occurred between us. I had to deny what felt natural and helpful to me.

Gestalt is more than a set of experiments. It is a way of living, a way of understanding life and relationships in the here and now.

What Gestalt offers to pastoral carers is a framework of thought that values the experiences of yourself and the person with whom you share caring equally. Gestalt is not a series of techniques or a formula for change. Gestalt is not a way to "open people up." Gestalt is a way of understanding relationships and change that validates experience in the here and now, as well as a person's history and life experience. Gestalt is a way of seeing value in the difficulties that persons face and sometimes overcome.

For me, the theory is eternal. From a Christian perspective, it illustrates life, death, and resurrection: a way of living a part of our lives, allowing parts of our lives to die, and resurrection to occur and support a new form of "doing life" to be developed.

I hope you find the journey interesting, fun, and "figure building."

A STATEMENT OF THEOLOGY

This theological statement is written from the perspective of my primary ministry: Pastoral Counseling. Any references to "clients" and "counseling" could also relate to "members" and "pastoral caring" as well.

Speaking from my here and now, I am a Christian, believing in Jesus Christ as the Incarnation of God, as my Savior and Lord. I believe that in His life, Christ demonstrated the values that God calls for all of us to strive toward. In the person of Jesus, God announced the participation of the Creator with the Creation, affirmed the talents and skills of all persons, and provided a model of and for relationships.

I view my ministries as those of Pastoral Counselor and Pastoral Theologian. Each has a specific task. The task of pastoral theology is, to quote Thomas C. Oden:

> [to seek] to give clear definition to the tasks of ministry and enable its improved practice. Because it is a pastoral discipline, pastoral theology seeks to join the theoretical with the practical. . . . Yet it is not merely a theoretical statement or objective description of what occurs in ministry. . . . Its proximate goal is the improved practice of ministry.[5]

I fulfill this in many ways. One task in ministry is to re-present in a living and touchable way the values of faith. I cannot represent God in the true sense.

Representatives, by definition, may only speak the words of the one they represent. Indeed, they must divorce themselves from their own language and experience, and communicate only with the words and actions of the persons for whom they are communicating.

My task is to re-present to the persons I provide care the values of faith that incorporate myself and my relationship with God and Jesus Christ. I re-present through the sharing of myself in my personal participation with the client. I participate with them, exploring and experiencing life from a perspective of value and faith. Pastoral caring is, indeed, a ministry of relationship and participation.

---

*The task—your task—is to develop and nurture **your personal way** of representing faith to others.*

These relationships are characterized by participation with others in their struggle for wholeness and identity. These relationships are grounded in the affirmation of a person's worth in being a member of God's world, accented by his or her desire and work to gain self-understanding. Pastoral caring is grounded in the belief that God accepts and affirms our entire human nature.

I am a pastor whose ministry is that of caring. It is my relationship as pastor, as well as counselor, that distinguishes me from others in a client's helping system. Being a pastor is part of my personal identity and a filter through which I view, and do, ministry.

I believe that it is the work of the Holy Spirit and myself that allows insights to be realized and change to take place through the caring process. These changes take place not only through the actions, words, and learnings of pastoral caring. Rather, these elements of caring are transformed through the Spirit from simple words and actions, to words and actions of faith.

As God views all persons in their totality, so I strive to view persons as whole. As Jesus did not view a person's needs, hurts, and celebrations isolated from their whole existences, neither can I as one who re-presents God.

Process theology accents this view of the whole in pastoral caring. It accents the experience of the person, the client, and consists of experiences of life too numerous to mention. Each person and each experience is of value. Process theology compares the realities of both carer and client. It asks:

> Is the carer seeing another kind of reality? Is he or she seeing the other as a center of activity, pulsating with life, ceaselessly forming and reforming [themselves] hundreds of times in the single hour they are together . . . Is the carer seeing [them] as a person, a Thou, not static, but a dynamic center of feeling, aiming, imagining, wishing, aspiring, fighting, surrendering activity? And does not the carer sense that he or she, too, is a person constantly experiencing the multiplicity of life so that there are never two fractions of time exactly alike?[6]

It is the process view, valuing the experience of both the carer and client, that makes its incorporation into pastoral theology critical. If each person is valuable, if each person shares experiences, then the shared life experience of carer and client must be considered.

My clients are part of a larger system of expectations, history, and images. I am part of their system, and must work to understand their inner workings and meanings, as well as the "we" that is created through our relationship.

Theology and the Therapeutic Relationship

I view pastoral care and counseling as a response to the account of the paralytic being lowered through the roof. Many persons' lives are paralyzed by fear, hopelessness, and helplessness. Jesus lived amongst them just as pastoral carers do today. Jesus was close enough to this man to be struck by the debris of the ceiling as it was removed, as well as emotionally close enough to feel the debris of this man's life. Pastoral counselors are too present with people as they address the issues of life that paralyze them. As a result, they experience both the joy and the fear that change can create.

All people are in the process of becoming; the recognition of this process is central to understanding the process of change. We are all in the process of becoming.

Persons who come to me are in the "process of becoming." It is my role as a pastoral counselor to be with them in the course of their struggle. Anton Boisen, the founder of Clinical Pastoral Education wrote:

> The priest or minister at [their] best brings to the task of helping the distressed in mind certain insights . . .
>
> [They] recognize the deep longings of the human heart and the significance of the constructive forces which are manifest alike in the religious conversion experience and in acute mental illness. [They] recognize the fundamental need of love, and the dark despair of guilt and estrangement from those we love, and the meaning of forgiveness through faith in the Love that rules the universe and in whose eyes no one is condemned who is in the process of becoming better . . . In such insights lies the important contribution of the competent minister of religion more than in any particular technique.[7]

Richard Dayringer states:

> The purpose of a theology of Relationship is to make persons aware of their relationship to God as Creator. Such a theory is quite relevant, because no part of life is beyond its reach; it assumes that the activities of all people are important to God. The theory of relationships is not remote from real life. It is engaged in the day-to-day struggle of persons to find meaning in the multiplicity of selves, the turmoil of human relationships, and the encounter with the cosmic forces that surround them.[8]

John Patton has expressed: "If any healing occurs through pastoral counseling, it occurs through relationship."[9]

Clients desire a change in their lives, and a participant with them in the process of and for change. Perhaps, as some do, they seek a style of care and counseling that is distinctively pastoral and will affirm their personal religious and spiritual roots.

Perhaps they feel a spiritual part of their lives is missing, and they desire counseling that will nurture this. Or, perhaps, they desire counseling and just happened upon a pastoral counselor. The fact is, they are here for change. William Oglesby wrote:

> As we have seen, such pastoral care is not concerned primarily with producing right knowing or right doing, although neither of these is ignored. Rather, there is throughout the basic intention of reestablishing broken relationships, of healing wounds of loneliness and grief, of loving and forging in the context of truth and grace.[10]

Persons who seek care desire change—to become better or different persons than they are. They long to be in the process of change. Jacob Firet notes:

> He is no static God in the sense of the philosophers. Jehovah is always active, always dynamically here, in this world. The Hebrew does not say that Jehovah *is,* or that Jehovah exists, but that he *does.* Properly speaking, the Hebrew verb *hayah* does not mean 'to be' so much as 'to come to be.' Hebrew has no real verb of 'being' but one of 'becoming.' The verb is active and not static.[11]

People, too, struggle with their sense of "being" or becoming. People enter pastoral care and counseling relationships because they are in a process, on a journey.

They are engaged in an exodus experience from the land filled with former ideas and beliefs and are on the move toward a new land. This land may not be filled with milk and honey, and almost surely the journey there will not always be sweet. However, in the process of becoming, they have a companion: the pastoral counselor or other carer.

Inherent within pastoral care and counseling is an awareness of the covert and overt religious language and symbols of persons.

These words and symbols become a vehicle for understanding the person, and their understanding of the Holy. Within pastoral caring is an awareness of the healthy desire and movements people have toward life and the decisions of life made out of fear or defensiveness.

It is the integration of sound psychological understandings, the affirmation and development of personally held faith values, and an understanding of a person's life and religious heritage that creates the distinctive nature of pastoral care and counseling. It is the integration of ideas, of experience and faith, not the isolation of the person through diagnostic terms, that creates the medium through which change can take place.

---

*The distinction of pastoral care and counseling is the affirmation and inclusion of faith into the care of lives. It is within the bounds of the **pastoral relationship** that change is supported and takes place.*

Pastoral care and counseling is not the infliction of specific religious values or ideologies; rather, pastoral caring includes the exploration of the religious values of the client. Pastoral caring includes finding a more complete meaning of life through the appreciation and utilization of these values and themes of life.

These values may or may not be identified as religious by the client. The pastoral counselor, however, hears and sees with the concept of faith as a primary tool for understanding. Carroll Wise states:

> The essence of therapy is rather in helping a person discover the depths of [their] own being and express this in symbols that carry vital meaning. Technical language, theological or psychological, has little or no place in therapy. Living religious language does have a place, and by this meant language that picks up and expresses vital experiences with which the person is struggling. Persons who have read books, (students for example) often try to explain themselves in the language of a book that has impressed them, but this is defensive . . . But the

essence of therapy—and of redemption, is an intuitive and empathetic relationship where a person is encouraged to discover their real self and express its meaning for [their lives] in terms that are vital and viable.[12]

Through the mutual understanding of these connections between life experience and faith, the momentum toward a goal for change is created. The values of the client create the framework around which the goals of the person's life are shaped. The process of pastoral care and counseling affirms the process as well as the goals.

Pastoral counseling includes perceiving a person's life difficulties from beyond the diagnostic criteria, to the effects these difficulties have had upon relationships with others, the world, themselves, and God. Pastoral counseling asks the ultimate questions of self-worth, acceptance, forgiveness, hope, and change. Pastoral care and counseling includes the death of former ideas and ideals, and the birth of new concepts, as well as the validation and continuation of some: Birth-Death-Resurrection.

Process theology speaks of the past, the moment, satisfaction, and the future. In essence, the birth of a new idea, the death of an old, and the incorporation in the future. Each person is in a constant process of:

> . . . creating and re-creating, determining and re-determining, realizing and re-realizing . . . The human being, like one type of creation, is an organism of incredible activity.[13]

Just as clients share their personal narratives as vehicles for self-understanding, I believe that Biblical narratives provide for us a vehicle for understanding the role, theology, and function of pastoral caring.

I view three narratives of Jesus' ministry as central in understanding my concept of ministry in and of pastoral caring. These narratives are: The Woman with the 12-Year Hemorrhage, the Story of Legion, and the Woman at the Well.

The Woman with the 12-Year Hemorrhage

Among them was a woman who had suffered from hemorrhages for twelve years; and in spite of long treatments by many doctors on which she had spent all she had, there had been no improvement; on the contrary, she had gotten worse. She had heard what people were saying about Jesus, so she came up from behind in the crowd and touched his cloak; for she had said to herself, "If I touch even his cloak I shall be cured." And there and then the source of her hemorrhages dried up and she knew in herself she was cured of her trouble. At the same time, Jesus, aware that power had gone out of him, turned round in the crowd and asked, "Who touched my clothes?"[14]

This is a model of contrasts between the lack of participation and understanding by the people of power and authority, and the participation of Jesus. The story depicts the desire of the woman for connection and participation with a person she believed not only cared, but who viewed her as whole and understood her struggle and desire for wholeness.

This woman was, from the perspective of her culture, perpetually unclean. The people the society affirmed and accepted for help and guidance provided her with prescriptive actions. They gave to her guidance for things to say and procedures to follow. Instead of accentuating her value, they emphasized their belief in her unworthiness and incompleteness. From the perspective of the leaders, if the prescriptions did not create healing, the blame for her continued uncleanness rested upon her. Her relationship with Jesus differed from that with the cultural religious leaders. She knew of his reputation, and the image portrayed by others. She knew of his message of wholeness and hope. These understandings created a different perspective on the relationship possible between herself and Jesus.

People struggle to find relationship. The help society offers is too often based upon doing . . . pastoral caring focuses upon being.

Although Jesus did not know her, his relationship with her was marked by effort and intention. Theirs was a relationship that left him exhausted, noted by his being "aware that power had left him."

It was a relationship not of convenient distance, but of tiring proximity. The message Jesus proclaimed drew the woman to him, and the action of living this message tired him.[15]

The task of pastoral care and counseling is to allow proximity to be created, where both counselor and client have the opportunity to share story and strength. The caring relationship is not built upon distance, but upon the closeness of working to understand the deeper meanings of clients' stories, the power of their pain over their lives, and their hope for change.

The Story of Legion

So they came to the other side of the lake into the country of the Gerasenes. As He stepped ashore, a man possessed by an unclean spirit came up to him from among the tombs where he had been dwelling. He could no longer be controlled; even chains were useless; and he had often been fettered and chained up, but he had snapped his chains and broken the fetters. No one was strong enough to master him. And so, unceasingly night and day, he would cry aloud among the tombs on the hillsides and cut himself with stones. When he saw Jesus in the distance, he ran and flung himself down before him, shouting loudly, "What do you want with me Jesus, Son of the Most High God? In God's name, do not torment me." Jesus asked him, "What is your name?" "My name is Legion," he said, "for there are so many of us." And he begged that Jesus would not send them out of the country. . . . .

[The people] came to Jesus and saw the mad-man who had been possessed by the Legion of devils, sitting there clothed in his right mind; and they were afraid.[16]

Legion lived in true isolation. Possibly a renegade pig salesman, (after all, he was living alone, surrounded by pigs, not the most desired position in life in a Jewish land) he lived amid the tombs. He had gone crazy. There were no opportunities for relationships, no people to hear his story, and no one to participate with him in life and give him hope.

The demon himself proclaims the identity of Jesus as "Jesus, Son of the Most High God." In these few words, he identifies Jesus as the one who bears the salvation of humanity, the one who comes from God.[17,18]

Jesus proclaimed hope through his acceptance of Legion. Jesus made the simple statement, "Tell me your story." As a result in the sharing of his story, Legion's history–his life–was affirmed, and his isolation ended. He had an opportunity to live not in isolation, but in relationship. The simple act of relating provided hope for him, and the message of wholeness, despite the views of others or his history. Although the world viewed Legion as crazy, God called Legion whole.

Pastoral caring provides an opportunity for a person to move from isolation through the telling of his or her story. The act of telling the story creates a Holy Ground where counselees are illuminated and defined not by the images others have placed upon them, but by the value God places upon each of us. By experiencing stories from a pastoral view, clients can come to understand themselves from a view of relational hope, not isolating fear.

The Woman at the Well

> The disciples had gone away to the town to buy food. . . .
> Meanwhile, a Samaritan woman came to draw water. Jesus
> said to her, "Give me a drink." The Samaritan woman said,
> "What do you, a Jew, ask a drink of me, a Samaritan woman?"
> [Jews and Samaritans, it should be noted, do not use vessels in
> common.] Jesus answered her, "If only you knew what God
> gives, and who it is that is asking you for a drink, you would
> have asked him and he would have given you living water." At
> that moment his disciples returned, and were astonished to
> find him talking with a woman; but none . . . of them said,
> "What do you want?" or "Why are you talking with her?"[17]

This story contains a surprise ending to a common story. There had been enmity between the Jews and Samaritans for generations. Custom and tradition provided clear lines of separation between the two cultures and their peoples. The Jews and the Samaritans were to have no contact; and yet here they did. In this moment, Jesus gave to her the same respect as he would give anyone. Jesus became the new advent for new relationships between nations and people.[20]

In this narrative, Jesus as the Logos–the Word made flesh–makes all things and all relationships new. Jesus' presence and words do not heal an illness or a madness: they cure a relationship between people and God, and bring the two together.

The power of the spoken word (the Logos–the Word made flesh) is real. The words spoken cannot be separated from the actions of ministry. The narrative also depicts the intentional actions of Jesus in making his presence and message known to the woman.

These narratives illustrate themes that are central to both my theology and practice of pastoral care and counseling. First, relationship is the key element in pastoral counseling. It is not enough to master theological ideas, counseling insights, or techniques. Without a relationship that affirms the individual's wholeness even amidst their brokenness, he or she will not experience the meaning or message of pastoral care and counseling.

Second, through the telling of the client's story, the true vehicle of understanding is provided for both the counselor and client. Incorporated within the story are the meanings a person places upon life, as well as his or her religious symbols and ideas.

The pastoral relationship, a relationship marked by acceptance and empathy, coupled with the telling of the story, allow for insights into the questions the client faces and for which he or she seeks resolution. Together, the relationship and story create the avenue for change, and the trust to be guided into new ways of living.

Third, pastoral care and counseling is effort. It is not simply listening for "God talk" or using words that sound religious. Pastoral caring includes hearing the ultimate questions of meaning and life, and the creation of responses to them. As counselors, pastoral counseling includes the effort in understanding our own place and journey of faith and learning of ourselves through the effort and experience of relationship.

A story from my residency in pastoral care and counseling follows: Pastoral care is like working with clay. In time, the client trusts you enough to share his or her soul with you. It is soft, pliable, like clay. Together, you view it from different perspectives, like clay, and then reshape it. Finally, the soul is returned to the client.

Like all soft clay, some remains on your hands. That clay, that bit of the person's soul-filled story, is yours to keep. It is the part of the person that will always remain with you. It, and the person, become part of *your* story.

NOTES

1. Gordon E. Jackson, *Pastoral care and process theology* (Lanham, MD: University Press of America, Inc., 1981), xii.

2. Jill S. Scharff and David E. Scharff, *Scharff notes: A primer of object relations therapy* (Northvale, NJ: Jason Aronson, Inc., 1992).

3. Frederick Perls, Ralph Hefferline, and Paul Goodman, *Gestalt therapy: Excitement and growth in human personality* (London: Souvenir Press, Ltd., 1951), 1.

4. James S. Simikin and Gary M. Yontiff, "Gestalt Therapy," in *Current psychotherapies,* edited by Raymond J. Corsini (Itasca, IL: F.E. Peacock Publishers, 1984), 279.

5. Thomas C. Oden, *Pastoral theology: Essentials of ministry* (San Francisco: Harper and Row Publishers, 1985), x-xi.

6. Gordon E. Jackson, *Pastoral care and process theology* (Lanham, MD: University Press of America Inc., 1981), 1-2.

7. Anton E. Boisen, *The exploration of the inner world* (New York: Harper and Brothers, 1936), 285.

8. Taken from *The Heart of Pastoral Counseling* by Richard Dayringer. Copyright © 1989 by Richard Dayringer. Used by permission of Zondervan Publishing House, 26.

9. John Patton, *Pastoral counseling: A ministry of the church* (Nashville: Abingdon Press, 1983), 30.

10. William B. Oglesby Jr., *Biblical themes for pastoral care* (Nashville: Abingdon Press, 1987), 41.

11. Jacob Firet, *Dynamics in pastoring* (Grand Rapids, MI: William B. Erdmans Publishing Company, 1986), 21.

12. Carroll A. Wise, *Pastoral psychotherapy* (New York: Jason Aronson Inc., 1983), xii.

13. Jackson, 4-7.

14. New English Bible © Oxford University Press and Cambridge University Press, 1961, 1970.

15. Oglesby, 196.

16. Mark 5:1-10, 15, NEB.

17. Reginold H. Fuller, *Studies in theology: A critical introduction to the New Testament* (Letchworth, Hertfordshire, England: Duckworth, 1971), 84-87.

18. Paul J. Achtemeir, *Proclamation commentaries: Mark* (Philadelphia: Fortress, 1975), 35.

19. John 4:8-10, 27, NEB.

20. Rudolf Bultman, *The gospel of John: A commentary* (Philadelphia: The Westminster Press, 1971), 178-180.

PART I:
THE LANGUAGE OF GESTALT

Chapter 1

Here and Now

Whatever is actual is, regardless time, always in the present. Whatever happened in the past *was* actual then, just as whatever occurs in the future *will* be actual at that time, but what *is* actual—and thus *all* that you can be aware of—must be in the present. Hence the stress, if we wish to develop the feeling of actuality, on words such as "now" and "at this moment." ... Likewise, what is actual for *you* must be where you are. Hence the stress on words like "here." You cannot at this moment experience any event—that is, live through it first-hand—if it takes place beyond the range of your receptors. You may imagine it, yes, but that means picturing it to yourself, and the picturing will be *here* where you are.[1]

Our interest in the satisfaction of needs does not imply a philosophy of hedonism. It merely states that if the individual is aware of what goes on inside of him and does something about it, he will feel better about himself than the person who does not possess the awareness or postpones satisfying himself.[2]

Gestalt therapy emphasizes not that we live for the moment, but that we live *in* the moment; not that we meet our needs immediately, but that we are present for ourselves in the environment.[3]

What Is the Concept of Here and Now and Why Is It Important to Gestalt Theory?

The concept of here and now is a foundation piece in the gestalt frame of reference. In gestalt terms, the here and now is where awareness, indeed life, occurs. Joseph Zinker wrote, "Primacy of the present experience means the focus of attention is on the moment-to-moment experience of the individual."[4] The concept is that simple.

The work of pastoral caring does not occur in the past or in the future. The work of pastoral caring occurs in the present relationship . . . "here and now."

The importance of the here and now concept cannot be stressed enough. Experiences are always *now*. What is happening is always *now*. This experiment may help bring the concept to life for you.

Get comfortable in your chair. Become aware of how the chair feels. How does your back contour to it? What does the fabric feel like? What does the chair seat feel like? All of these awareness questions are in the here and now. You can answer them easily. Now, think of another chair you sat in today. What did it feel like? How did your back contour to it? How did the seat feel? All of these questions focus not upon experiences of the *now*. Instead, they are of memory. The experiences of the past are not as immediately powerful as experiences of the present.

We live in the here and now. People who seek our help are frequently unaware of the here and now. Our task, from a gestalt perspective, is to help them become aware of the here and now so their lives can be lived more fully.

Does the "Here and Now" Idea Discount the Person's Past History?

It can seem like that. However, the concept does not discount history. Indeed, working in the here and now can facilitate a more personal evaluation of a person's history.

Your task, as a pastoral carer, is to aid persons in connecting their present experience with their life story. You can do this by supporting this exploration with questions such as: "Does this feel familiar?" and "What are you aware of right now, and does it feel familiar?" Let me provide an example.

You are speaking with a gentleman who is having difficulty accepting his aging process. As he is speaking, you mention to him that his eyes seem moist. He begins to speak of his sadness, and that he does not know where it comes from. You ask, "Does it feel familiar?" "Yes," he replies, "I feel like I did when my father died. And he died so young."

In this case, it was the work in the here and now that allowed this man to access the memory from the past that helped create order in his present. In this way, the work of the present creates the foundation for the appreciation of memories.

Should the Language I Use Also Be in the Here and Now?

Good question. The answer is yes . . . and then some. The language you use needs to be present and personal. For example, allow yourself to experience the difference between these two scenarios:

You are telling a friend of a painful experience in your life. He or she appears to be listening, and replies, "It's sad."

In the second scenario, you are telling the same story. This time, however, your friend states, "I feel sad as you tell me this," or perhaps, "My eyes are tearing."

What is different for you? The first scene is rather depersonalizing. The scene speaks of an almost nonhuman, "I/It" relationship. Gestalt emphasizes the "I/Thou"–person to person, me to you. The impact of your story on me. My tears as my response to your story.

This may seem like a small point. However, try it out for a few days. See how it feels to you. It may feel more risky—because it is more revealing of you. Try it out, and experience yourself more fully.

Some Ideas for Your Growth

Pay attention to the language our culture uses. Do we speak in the here and now, or do we often miss the mark? When people speak with you, do you feel the most connected when they speak in the here and now, or in another fashion?

NOTES

1. Frederick Perls, Ralph F. Hefferline, and Paul Goodman, *Gestalt therapy: Excitement and growth in the human personality* (London: Souvenir Press, 1951), 31, 33.

2. Joseph Zinker, *Creative process in gestalt therapy* (New York: Vintage Books, 1977), 94.

3. Zinker, 95.

4. Zinker, 162.

Chapter 2

Process versus Content

What Does Process versus Content Mean, and How Does It Effect My Use of Gestalt Theory?

The concept highlights how we "track" what happens in an exchange, and what we pay attention to. Paying attention to "content" means paying attention to each item as it is being discussed. It is "content based."

On the other hand, attending to "process" means paying attention to the meanings of what is being said. It is, in essence, being aware of, or attending to, what is not always immediately seen. "Process" can entail being aware of words, messages, inflection of voice, physical (body) process, and more.

I use music as an image to understand process and content. Imagine seeing or hearing a piece of music one note at a time. You only experience one note, after note, after note. There is no sense of connection, of differences—just notes. Now, imagine seeing or hearing the notes as they are intended. This time, tempo, dynamics, and other unique characteristics are experienced. This is process.

So, content can be understood as experiencing things in relative isolation. Essentially, paying equal attention to each item. Process, on the other hand, includes experiencing the flow, message, and sometimes even the unspoken message.

I have sometimes thought that when I am tracking in a process fashion, I am aware of experiencing the event. I can feel it, experience it, seemingly from the inside out. When I track in a content fashion, I lose energy and get caught up in the drama of the moment.

One way to illustrate process versus content is to imagine a church meeting. The meeting begins; it ends. Along the way, many "things" are talked about, but little appears to get accomplished. The meeting ends, and you ask yourself the questions, "What happened? What did the meeting mean?" The content probably was tracked fully. Items, things, were talked about individually. However, the meaning behind all that was discussed may have been lost.

To pay attention to the "process" of the meeting would mean paying attention to the flow of the ideas and allowing concepts to surface. Paying attention to process allows you to track the connections between topics discussed and find their common meaning. One marker of process thinking is the seemingly miraculous ability to say, "I sense that what we are talking about here is. . . . " or "I experience a theme to our work today . . . ." People will think you can read minds. They will think you are brilliant, and all you have done is state the painfully obvious.

You witness this concept frequently when working with couples in distress. You sit with them and witness their talking about "this and that." "Well, he did . . . " "Well, she did . . . " They are focusing upon content and would like you to do the same.

Just as Legion, we do not desire to live in isolation. By focusing upon the moment, we link ourselves with the people in our midst, the people we are caring for in the moment. This is the heart and soul of pastoral caring . . . and gestalt.

When you experience the unfolding drama from a "process" perspective, you are able to experience the exchange, paying attention to all that occurs. The words that are used, the way they are said, the body position, and the change in communication styles all become important. You begin to understand the message behind what is being communicated.

Process allows you to experience and to share your own experience. It creates a living process. Tracking process allows you to be with the people, while tracking content allows you to observe the people. Being in the process allows you to be in the flow of the issue, and often not the "things" of the discussion.

Does Focusing on the Process Cause One to Ignore What People Say?

It may seem like that. In reality, you are listening to their message, not *just* the words they say. You are listening to the whole message, not only the parts that make up the message. Tracking process can allow you to identify the contrast between what is said and what is communicated in a fuller form.

Tracking process can also help focus the work of the moment. Many times when I have given process feedback to people, the energy in the room seems to level off, and the people are able to communicate on an even playing field in the moment.

I remember a couple who would argue heatedly in their session. They had detailed memories of past fights as if they were on videotape. Each could outdo the other when it came to recalling "who said what to who and why." After many moments of hearing what was being said and allowing myself to experience it, I said, "I am aware that the more you talk, the louder each of you gets."

By my simply noting the process of the session, and a hunch, they were able to shift to some communication around desiring to be listened to. Each noted their fear of not being heard. Each felt they "had" to speak louder. Had I focused only upon what was said, I would have helped solve situational difficulties, but not the process, the meaning that lived under it. By attending to the process, they were able to make contact with each other from a point of commonality—the moment.

So, yes, it may seem that by focusing upon process you do not listen. In fact, you are listening *more* fully.

Chapter 3

Figure/Ground

A generation ago, gestalt psychology, an importation from Germany, made a scientific stir in this country. By ingenious experiments, it demonstrated many previously overlooked aspects of "visual perception." Scouting the notion that in seeing something, one collects visual fragments and assembles them into the object seen, it insisted that seeing is organized from the start—that is, it is a gestalt, or configuration. One's visual field is structured in terms of "figure" and "background".... Figure is the focus of interest—an object, pattern, etc.—with "ground" the setting or context.[1]

Individuals perceive the environment as a total unit of meaning, responding to the whole of what is seen. This whole is composed of the stimuli to which the persons attend directly, and those to which they do not attend directly. Focused attention organizes environmental parts into a visual whole, a gestalt that emerges as a figure dominating a field of impressions.[2]

The healthy individual is able to clearly experience and differentiate something in his foreground which interests and captivates him from that which is uninteresting. He experiences the sharpness and clarity of the figure, with little interest in a homogenized ground. In disturbed individuals, there is a confusion between figure and ground. There is a lack of purpose and focusing, so that as they look at a particular situation, they are not able to pick out what is central for them, that which has importance for them. From one moment to the next, they are unable to separate the important things for themselves from the unimportant things.[3]

What Is "Figure/Ground" and What Is Its Place in Gestalt Theory?

The concept of "figure/ground" is central to understanding how Gestalt is done. It is simple and at the same time, complex. The best way to understand figure/ground is, in true Gestalt fashion, to experience it. Ground yourself in your chair, and close your eyes. When you open them, be aware of what you focus upon. Notice it clearly. That is your "figure." Now, pay attention to what lies around your figure. Perhaps you are looking at a lamp on a table. It is your figure. The "ground" might be the table itself, the room, the rug, or even the house in which you are sitting.

Take a moment and reflect upon this concept. In essence, life is full of figure/ground experiences. We walk into a room, gaze about, and find the face we are seeking. That face is the figure and all else is ground. You are reading a newspaper article. The opening paragraphs provide the background (the ground) for the story (the figure). Later, the story itself may become the ground for another story.

But, you may ask, why is this concept so important?

Let me tell you a story. When I was growing up in Boston, John Hancock Insurance was building a new 67-story office building. The problem was, the windows kept popping out of it, sailing across Copley Square. No one was able to work in the building. Needless to say, pedestrians quickly learned about ducking for cover.

The city council told them to either fix the problem, or raze the building. First, John Hancock had to understand the problem with the building. They determined the building's shape was the source of the difficulty. The building was shaped like a narrow triangle. When the wind blew, as it often did in that part of the city, the building warped, the window frames warped, and quicker than you could say "duck," the windows went flying.

The problem was solved when Hancock installed rubber window frames that could take the twist. The problem could have been solved earlier if the foundation had been wider and the building had more ground on which to stand. In gestalt terms, "There was not enough ground to support the figure."

Ground is the foundation for any work that is done. Without enough ground, the idea being discussed, the change hoped for, or the solution to be developed, may fall flat.

SO GROUND ALWAYS COMES BEFORE FIGURE?

Yes, the ground is the first focus of our attention. In the concept of figure/ground, the figure is the focus of the ground. The ground builds up to "it," the figure.

Don't move too quickly to a figure. Allow solid ground to be developed to support your work . . . your figure. It may be tempting to cheer, "I found the figure." Instead, wait; you may have simply added, importantly, to the ground.

Can You Have More Than One Figure at a Time?

Well, you can try, but it gets confusing. Figures need time and space to be developed. Figures take energy. If more than one is being developed, insufficient energy or attention can be placed on them. Each may fade "back to ground" for lack of supportive ground. Only one figure can truly be supported at any one time.

Reflect upon a meeting where there seemed to be much confusion over what was being discussed. That is what happens when there are too many figures, basically more than one, being focused upon at a time. At the same time, a meeting where much is said, but nothing is accomplished can also be a sign of much ground being cultivated, but no figures being grown out of it.

Can You Show This in Operation?

The application of the concept takes practice. You do it every day. The task is to become aware of what it is you are doing. Your task is to pay attention, attend to the themes and process of what is said, or help shape the figure as supported by the ground. Your task is to listen and be aware of the ideas or themes that keep coming up.

Your task is to be aware of the focus of the energy—that is the location of the figure. Your task is to be interested.

Imagine you are at a church meeting. An idea is introduced, perhaps to change the color of the church social room. You could move directly to the decision process, "Okay folks, the idea has been raised to repaint the social room. What colors should we use?" You might get a decision. People might answer the question. However, there may not be a great emotional investment on their part. Why? There was not enough ground developed, and thus little energy focused.

If in the course of the discussion people spoke about the history of the room, who paid for it, and why it was built, you would have more ground. "Hmmm . . ." you might say, "I wonder what they are driving at?" Could they be talking about be the meaning of the room for the people? That might be the figure to explore in order to create more ground for a decision. If this figure was developed, the people might have the focused energy to move ahead and "own" the idea of painting "their" room.

Imagine a pastoral counseling session. A young man is discussing his fears of getting older. He is 35 years old and afraid of dying. You could provide some support, "You're young. You've got years ahead of you." In this interaction, you might not make clear "contact" with the person and the meaning his fears have for him. Insufficient ground was developed to make contact. Also, you have tracked the "content" and not the "process" of his exchange.

Ground could be developed by exploring the material he presents: his family, his life experiences, or what it is like for him in the here and now. This ground development may allow a figural issue to surface and be explored.

Again, follow the *process,* not solely the content of the exchange and help shape the experience. Attend to yourself and your process, as well as the process, of the other person.

This became clear to me several years ago when I was visiting a young man in our emergency room. He was 38 years old and was being admitted for chest pain. Nothing seemed to be wrong with him; all the tests were negative. Still, he had chest pain. As we spoke, I learned of his father's death years before. His father was 38 when he died, and had died during the current season of the year.

As the figure grew from the ground, the man began to cry and share the pain of his loss. His chest pains went away. Without the development of the ground–the foundation–the figure of his father's death and his present experience would have not been developed. Had I moved too quickly to my hunch of the father's connection, the figure would not have been supported. The figure would have remained the chest pain, not the young man's process. Our discussion would have remained focused upon "content," not on "process."

"All" I did was attend to process, showing interest in his story and aiding in the development of a "full fat figure" to experience.

Worship may be the best example of figure/ground development. In theory, as the time of worship moves ahead, each part builds upon the other: the Call to Worship is the ground for service; the Scripture is the ground for the sermon; and the Hymns, the ground for the service theme.

Take the time to examine your worship life from the perspective of figure/ground; imagine how it is better to build the experience from "ground" up. Ever wonder why a service felt flat? Perhaps your ground was not developed fully. Perhaps there was too much ground, and no figure.

In some respects, the "chit-chat" that seems so meaningless in many pastoral settings has great meaning. It contains the ground for future figures. Listening to someone may become the ground for a figure of trust in you. The seemingly senseless conversation about a child's graduation may be the ground for a discussion about parenting. The conversation about an ill pet may become the ground for a later figure around trusting you. If you take in the concept of figure/ground fully, the connection between all of life is nearly endless.

Are There Pitfalls to Watch Out For?

Yes, there are two: hanging on to figure or ground too long, or not long enough.

Imagine figure/ground being like a wave. The wave begins to form–ground–finally, it takes shape–figure–then falls away and becomes ground for the next wave. The cycle continues on and on.

All figures need to, and will, fall back into ground over time. Like death and resurrection, this process must be supported to occur naturally . . . not too soon and not too late.

Imagine if instead of this, either the building of the wave or the wave itself continued on. If the building continued, no wave, no focus of energy, would occur. If the wave did not break, its energy could not be given up for the next wave.

The key is to develop enough ground so a figure can be supported and not so much that staleness and fatigue begin to set in for lack of focus. At the same time, remaining on a figure too long can cause frustration and loss of momentum. That feeling of "We're done already!" needs to be affirmed.

I have found that a perceived decrease in energy *may* indicate a loss of direction and/or a loss of focus. Perhaps it is time to move on to the next topic allowing the figure to intentionally become ground for the next figure.

So, I Should Not Jump at the First "Figure" That I Experience?

Right. There are times when the first item discussed is indeed the figure to be focused upon. Usually, however, this is not the case. Even if the first item is the figure, ground still needs to be developed to support this quickly growing figure. Usually, the first figure you experience needs to be seen as ground for a figure.

Frequently, the first item discussed is the *effect* of the figure to be discussed. For example, being angry at someone may be the effect of having difficulty setting relational limits.

Figure/ground . . . the building block for all work from a gestalt perspective. Ground forms the foundation for the figure to stand upon. With insufficient ground, the figure is not supported and cannot be fully developed.

For Your Own Growth

In your daily living, pay attention to the figure/ground concept at work. Pay attention to the development of stories in any format. Pay attention not only to the figure/ground work, but also to what happens if they are not fully developed. Next, read a passage of Scripture. How is the ground developed? How are the figures known? Try the Parables, and follow the development of ground and figure.

NOTES

1. Frederick Perls, Ralph F. Hefferline, and Paul Goodman, *Gestalt therapy: Excitement and growth in the human personality* (Highland, NY: The Gestalt Journal Press), 1994, 272.

2. From Margaret P. Korb, Jeffrey Gorrell, and Vernon Van De Riet, *Gestalt Therapy: Theory and Practice.* Copyright ©1989 by Allyn and Bacon. Reprinted by permission.

3. Joseph Zinker, *Creative process in gestalt therapy* (New York: Vintage Books, 1977), 92.

Chapter 4

Attending

Gestalt therapy [as well as client-centered therapy, psychodrama, existential therapy, and logotherapy] takes a phenomenological stance in regards to the therapeutic relationship. That is, there is a belief that the therapist can work best with the client by entering into his or her phenomenological world, experiencing along with the client the client's perspectives. This orientation requires a close, personal relationship with the client. The therapist cannot be aloof, distant, or totally objective in interaction. The therapist, therefore, needs to be able to understand the client's personal feelings, beliefs, thoughts, and values in order to fully respond to those aspects of the client. The therapist must participate as well as observe.[1]

What Is Attending?

"Attending" is more than a word, and more than an action. Instead, it is a way of relating to others in an active and relational manner. It is at the heart of Gestalt work. Attending means, simply, paying attention to others, *as well as to ourselves.* The first concept, attending to others, makes sense, and is at the center of most perspectives on helping and is rather natural. The concept of attending to ourselves, however, is not as common and is frequently misunderstood. It is an element within the Gestalt approach that I feel lends itself well to pastoral caring.

In Gestalt, it is said that there are two stances of attending: receptive and active. The active stance is more Western in nature; it is more outward and active. The other stance, receptive, is more Eastern in nature; it relies more upon attending to ourselves. In many ways, our pastoral caring education has been based more upon the Western, outward stance, than on the inward Eastern stance. Gestalt provides a way to utilize both stances.

How Do I "Attend"?

Attending happens in many ways. Take a moment and reflect upon times when you have felt "connected" to someone. How did it happen? What data helped create your awareness? Perhaps it was how he or she looked at you. Perhaps the person appeared interested in what you were saying. Perhaps it was the body posture the individual took as you spoke. Perhaps he or she leaned forward and appeared highly interested, or leaned back, giving you some needed space. Perhaps the person even made sounds that felt connective: "hmm"s and "oh." Perhaps an interest was shown in you by asking you to elaborate. Perhaps the person gave you the great gift of silence.

Each of these actions, and countless others, are ways of being and of demonstrating an attentive and attending relationship with others. We all have our favorite, more developed, natural ways of demonstrating our interest.

But What About Attending to Ourselves?

For some people, attending to themselves is awkward and more risky than attending to others. Yet, it is important for all to do, most especially those in the helping professions.

Again, reflect upon a moment in your life when you felt very connected and attentive to another person. How did you know? Were your eyes tearful, or your breathing difficult? Did you find yourself leaning forward, and realizing you were drawn to the person and his or her story? What did you experience that created your awareness of being attentive to the person? What were your feelings? Were you happy, sad, interested, or even bored? What questions did you feel like asking?

Our individual style of being self-aware is part of attending to ourselves. One experiment you might try is to note what you attend to in music or art. Do you attend to lyrics, or music? Do you attend to colors, or shapes?

When you are with people, what do you attend to? Do you attend to their voices, their language, their clothing, or perhaps to their humor? Take the time to learn what you attend to naturally, and develop you attending skills more fully. At the same time, try leaning into other, less developed styles.

Attending to the other both develops and supports the relationship. Attending to ourselves deepens our relationship with ourselves, and as result, with all persons with whom we relate.

Each day of the week, attend to a different item in a different facet of life. You can do it in your work, in watching television—even the advertisements. Take the time to gain an awareness of how your experiences change when you attend to different events and experiences.

So, How Does All This Get Used?

The concept of "attending" becomes very visible in the figure/ground as well as process versus content. In general, attending is utilized to shape the work you are doing with another person, aiding by increasing the person's awareness of self, and of you.

I worked with a young woman a few years ago who stated she was unable to feel much. She would say she felt "cold and unfeeling." What I experienced as she spoke was a depth of feeling coming from her—only it was not in her words. Her eyes teared, but never cried. She would rub her forearms at times as she spoke and would lean forward in her chair, then quickly fall back.

In the midst of the session, I said simply, "Your eyes look moist." With that statement, she began to cry softly, and shifted her focus from the content of her story, to the process—her deep fear of feeling.

As she continued to speak, I noted, "I'm interested in the way you describe yourself." She seemed to gain some energy and went on sharing more details based not upon fact, but upon her personal understanding. Finally, as the session was drawing to a close, I stated, "I'm feel a tightness right here (pointing to my chest). I am touched by your story." She began to cry softly and said, "I didn't think anyone would really be interested."

All along the way, I gave her physical space when it seemed to be needed and more proximity when that seemed to be her need. I attended to herself and myself, to create a safe environment for maintaining a focus for her experiences.

What Exactly Were You Attending To?

I was attending to several things. First, I attended to her energy. I monitored this by paying attention to *where my interest was drawn.* I asked myself, "Where was her energy? What was she doing with it?" In this case, I was drawn to the energy in her eyes–her tears. I may have also been drawn to her lack of affect about her emotionally charged story. In that way, I might have said, "As you tell your story, your expression is not changing." In that manner, I would have brought her attention and her energy to another part of herself. Through it all, I believed that if I attended to both of us, I could help shape her figure/ground.

In many ways, attending seems almost too simple: Note what you experience and the work will naturally develop in the direction of a clear figure.

So, There Are Times To Be Both Receptive and Active in My Attending?

Yes. There are times to be each, and the task is to know which is needed when. As you can imagine, sharing too much awareness of the other person can cause overload. It can clutter the ground with too much "stuff." At the same time, sharing too much of your self-awareness can shift the focus of your pastoral work from the other to yourself.

In the example of the woman who felt "cold and unfeeling," had I chosen to provide all of the data I experienced (her arm-rubbing and chair-shifting), the focus would have shifted away from the process to what I call "content clutter." At the same time, I attended to my own feelings of sadness, and chose to share them with her in a way that supported *her* work. I chose not to share the story in my life that came to mind. (I dealt with that with my therapist.)

At all times, however, attending to yourself will aid in understanding others, even if you do not share it with them also. There is great value in acknowledging the sadness or joy you feel to yourself, and shape your work accordingly with that insight.

That's Fine, But How Can I Use It in Everyday Ministry?

Take a moment to reflect upon the actions of pastoral caring. How often do you find yourself searching for the "right" question to ask in order to help someone? How often do you wonder how to get a stalled meeting moving? What would happen if you stated, as is said in Gestalt, the painfully obvious—what was happening in the moment?

Imagine if in the midst of a counseling session, you felt at a loss and wondered what to say to someone who is in the midst of pain. Imagine the connection that might be created if you were to attend to the silence, and allow it to exist. Or imagine saying, "I'm aware that in the silence, your eyes have become brighter" or "I feel a holiness in our silence."

Imagine being at a meeting that seemed stuck, and simply stating, "I feel stuck." Or being at a meeting, feeling anxious over a discussion, and making that statement. What about sharing, "This topic feels very important to me," to validate the importance that exists. Imagine saying, "I've noticed that every time we get close to a decision, another idea pops up." This attitude of attending is very different from saying, "Let's move on."

The "how" of attending will become more clear as your learn more of Gestalt in the pages that follow.

I Notice That Statements Are Made in a First-Person Fashion. Is There Any Significance in This?

Yes. I am not an "it." To say, "It feels sad," is to make myself an it. A person cannot have a connection with me and my "it." Self-awareness, attending to ourselves, needs to be shared from ourselves: I feel; I sense.

The exception can be when you are sharing data you have noticed. For example, I might say, "I noticed as you said that, your eyes teared." I am more likely, however, to say, "As you said that, your eyes teared" or even, "Your eyes are moist," and leave off the "I noticed." This shortened form collects the energy more quickly. After all, you are not sharing an internal awareness; you are sharing an observation intended to quickly establish contact.

Some Ideas for Your Growth

To experience lack of attending, try this experiment. Begin speaking with someone about a belief that is very important to you. Ask this person, periodically, to look away from you and interrupt with his or her own ideas. Note in yourself the effect of when the person turns away and speaks over you.

In your own work, note the effect when you attend to others. If you feel disconnected from someone, you probably are. Try to reconnect with yourself and track the effect this has upon yourself and the other person.

Attending gives energy to your work. Attending requires both action and patience. Your development of your own ways of attending will shape and support your work.

Finally, what are your preferred ways of attending? Do you attend well with your eyes, your body posture, or your voice? Pay attention to how you attend, and try to balance your attending style with some variety.

NOTE

1. Margaret P. Korb, Jeffrey Gorrell, and Vernon Van De Reit, *Gestalt therapy: Practice and theory* (Needham Heights, MA: 1989), 110-111.

Chapter 5

The Whole Is Greater
Than the Sum of Its Parts

The foundation of the first principle of Gestalt therapy is holism. The essence of the holistic conception of reality is that all nature is a unified and coherent whole. . . . Holistically, we cannot understand ourselves by summing our understanding of our heart, our brain, our nervous system, our limbs, our circulatory system. We are not simply an accumulation of functions. The ordinary language expression of this is: The whole is greater than the sum of the its parts. "Greater" means different in quality form; it also refers to the entirety of the object or event. Therefore, the whole is a new event, as water is greater than two parts of hydrogen and one part oxygen, and a hand is greater than four fingers and a thumb.[1]

When I first moved to Ohio, I saw an advertisement on television. It began with a single black dot. Over the course of the ad, the camera panned back from this single black dot. It became larger and larger; and slowly I could tell what it was: a black bug. This was an ad for a bug killer for crops. It was an example of the holistic view of Gestalt. Black dot by black dot, it was just that: a bunch of black dots. As a whole, it was much more.

"Gestalt" is not directly translatable from its German roots to English. The closest translation is "The Whole." Gestalt calls us to be aware of the whole in any relationship, and that awareness in itself is a departure from much of our seminary training. It calls upon us to step back to get a full view–a whole view.

To focus upon the whole is to place value upon the totality of the other per-son's life . . . it is including yourself in their system . . . including all of their life in their system and affirming from this one point of view, the value of all of life experience.

You would think that as pastoral carers this would be natural for us, but it is not. Instead, we frequently find ourselves focused upon one aspect, one point, and miss the value of the whole.

I have noticed that some seminary students and graduates have difficulty with understanding, or perceiving, the whole in their car-ing. Although seminary pastoral caring classes do not focus primar-ily upon teaching technique and theory, students occasionally get in a pattern of asking questions. Clinical Pastoral Education, CPE, an intensive educational program in pastoral ministry, can accent this. Frequently, CPE case presentations, exchanges between carer and recipient are understood line by line, not as a congruent whole.

Being true to "the whole is greater than the sum of the parts" *allows us* to participate in learning the rhythm and meanings of people's whole lives, not just the elements of their lives. The whole is greater than the sum of the parts allows us to help others, our-selves, and become more aware of our individual lives and how they create a whole relationship in the here and now.

Does That Mean I Should Disregard the Individual Parts To Be More Aware of The Whole Person?

No, not by any means. Rather, it means that you remain aware of the meaning these parts may have in the whole story. In the practice of this concept, you remain aware of the parts, however, you aid the persons attending to the whole of themselves. In other words, the "parts" become the ground for the figure of the whole.

In Gestalt, one plus one equals more than two. Attending to the whole, not just the parts, values the entire experience that is occurring. By attending to the whole, you truly relate with what is . . . the ground for what is to become.

Some Ideas for Your Growth

In your daily life, attend to our culture's artificial division of people and groups into parts instead of whole bodies. Pay attention to what life is like *for you* to be viewed from only one limited perspective. Imagine what it is like for others.

NOTE

1. Joel Latner, *The gestalt therapy book* (Highland, New York: The Gestalt Journal Press, 1973), 4, 5.

Chapter 6

Being Aware

A common objection to Gestalt therapy is that it is altogether too self-conscious. It is maintained that people in therapy are already overly aware of what they are doing. What they need is to be able to give up some of this awareness so they can behave less self-consciously, with grace and spontaneity. At first glance, this objection makes sense. . . . The awareness which concerns us in gestalt are also those which help restore the unity of the individual and integrated function. Before he can alter his behavior in any way, the individual must first encompass the sensations and feelings which go along with it. Recovery of the acceptability of awareness—no matter what it may reveal—is a crucial step to the development of new behaviors . . . At its best, awareness is a continuous means of keeping oneself up to date.[1]

You Use the Phrase "Being Aware" Frequently.
Does This Have Some Special Significance in Gestalt?

To answer the question, let me invite you to try a small experiment. First, get comfortable in your chair: feet flat on the floor, arms by your sides. I want you to close your eyes and be aware of your experience.

As you sit, what do you hear, smell, and taste? What do you experience in your feet? In your hands? As you breathe, do you sense the clothing on your chest or the sound of your own breathing? Be aware.

Next, open your eyes and look around you. What are you aware of? What do you see? What colors are in the room? Where are the shadows? Be aware.

"Being aware" occurs through our senses. We "experience" awareness. Experience is a key word. It does not mean how we feel, exactly, or what we think, exactly. It means what happens within us: our body sensations, our emotions, our feelings, and even our thoughts.

Here is the difference between being fully aware and "just" feeling: you are speaking with someone in your office. He or she is telling you about a chronic illness. The individual begins to tear a bit and you ask, "How do you feel?" The reply is "Sad." This person, and you, have been culturally guided to an answer–feelings mean "happy, sad, mad, glad . . . "

---

*Awareness is more than feeling. It is **experiencing** ourselves as individuals and as part of a larger system. The experience is total . . . body, mind, and spirit.*

Imagine if instead you asked, "I'm wondering, what are you aware of, right now as we talk?" The reply might be, "I'm aware that my stomach is tied up in knots, and I'm crying. My arms are feeling like I want to hit something. I'm remembering how I felt when I was a kid, and they told me I'd never be tall enough for the basketball team. God, I hate that feeling. It's like I can't change the end result."

By asking someone to be aware, you "increase awareness" of what already is. This seemingly simple change in language and of focus "undoes" many cultural rules of what feelings and sensations we are "allowed" to feel and speak of to others. The simple request to "be aware" changes the person's point of focus from a part of oneself to all of oneself in the here and now.

At the same time, Gestalt encourages you, the carer, to be aware as well. From a Gestalt frame of reference, what you experience is part of the whole–the relationship between yourself and the other person. This "holism" within the relationship differentiates Gestalt from many other forms of counseling and understanding. For some, this difference is a thrill; to others, it is a threat.

Remember the example of the chronically ill person? Imagine the value of sharing *your* awareness with this individual. Imagine the value of sharing your feelings of sadness. Imagine your eyes tearing. In awareness, all of our senses are allowed to be experienced. All of ourselves becomes a vehicle for understanding, not just our "feelings."

How Might This Principle Be Used in Pastoral Caring?

Awareness can be used creatively in worship. Normally, we see the Communion elements; we might eventually taste them. Then again, if you are vision or taste impaired, this may not be true. You could heighten people's awareness by, perhaps, having grape aroma-producing wafers filling the room with the sweetness of grapes. You might even bake bread in the sanctuary. Imagine.

In spiritual development, you might ask people to become more aware of their hands as they pray. They might become more aware of the softness of their prayer positions, and want to make themselves more solid, or the other way around. Awareness can be used within pastoral counseling as you ask persons to be more aware of their tears, or how they experience a passage of comfort being read.

So, the Goal Is to Make People Become Aware?

Not exactly. As you will discover in later sections, the task of the pastoral carer is to provide the support and guidance that may allow people to become more aware of themselves and their environment.

It is through awareness that people can have a broader foundation from which to make decisions. So . . . you do not "make" someone become aware. You provide support and guidance so that the person might become more aware.

Awareness is a learned skill. Our culture equates feeling with awareness. This is not true. It is only by practicing awareness that we can capture the whole aspect of the concept. Over time, you become cognizant of becoming more aware.

It must also be remembered that people can only manage so much awareness at a time. It is not helpful, or wise, to continue increasing awareness. There is a toleration point after which people become overwhelmed. I am reminded of a friend in my Gestalt training program. After the holiday break, he shared with me that he had lost over one-half of his clients. It seems he had been focusing upon increasing their awareness without creating a way to rid themselves of the energy. They became so aware, they lost their ability to make contact with the process of growth and change. So, be careful when you attempt to increase others' awareness. Attend to their process.

NOTE

1. Erving Polster and Miriam Polster, *Gestalt therapy integrated: Contours of theory and practice* (New York: Vintage Books, 1973), 207-210.

Chapter 7

Theme

Theme is the organizer of our awareness. It includes our apperceptive mass—who/what we are on both a known and unconscious level and the structure which we create as we present ourselves to the world. It includes our combined apperceptive mass which is created when we join with others. It gives our lives meaning and coherence in what would otherwise be a buzz and whir or impressions and memories.[1]

What Is the Meaning of "Theme" in Gestalt Theory?

Theme can be described in many ways. Rainette Frantz, a founder and faculty member at the Gestalt Institute of Cleveland, states its meaning in various ways:

> Theme points the way that the session may take. . . . It integrates the session . . . In Gestalt, we view theme as schema or a screen through which we perceive our lives. They are the stories we tell ourselves in the dark of night, in the sometimes painful dawn to make some sense out of our experience.[2]

The late Dr. Tim LeBar, mentor and faculty member stated:

> [Theme is] . . . The organization of what's happening into a manageable unit . . . [it] unifies—establishes common figure/ground formation . . . They are not good or bad, right or wrong. All themes are OK . . . They are as such mutually agreed upon . . . Human lives have many themes. The amount of energy and the willingness should guide selection.[3]

What are themes? Themes are the threads that flow within a discussion. As Tim said, they unify the work that you are doing. Themes are developed; they grow out of the ground and the figures used. Themes are guides to our work. Themes are the whole made out of the parts and pieces presented. They may be understood on one level as the thread that unifies the work.

Are There Various Types of Themes?

Yes. Themes can have different points of focus: general or specific. Some themes speak to grand scale events such as world peace. Others may speak to minievents such as the best place to get a cheese steak sub in Dayton.

How Do You Identify Themes?

Themes are identified most easily by the energy and interest you sense. If you attend carefully to your daily experiences, themes are drawn into your awareness. They arise from the entire exchange—not only the words, but the inflection of the style of work as well. They rise from the figures of the experience.

For example, I had the opportunity to work with a young woman who began the session by stating she did *not* want to talk about her mother. So, as she *did* talk about her mother and then other persons, I noticed that the theme of the work was her difficulty in establishing and maintaining limits on relationships.

Essentially, she would allow others to define how she would relate with them. She would follow their advice and not her own. She would define herself by the terms of others. The theme was experienced by me in her words, and her style of hesitant statements about her participation and view of relationships. I noticed it in her willingness to follow my lead in session as well, seldom stating her view of the work. As you will learn later, she was being "confluent" in relationships.

As we worked, the focus was not upon the content of her story—her relationships with her mother, brother, and boyfriend. Instead, we attended to the theme, "I let others decide how I will relate to them."

Is Theme More Than Just the Thread of the Work?

Theme does mean more than just the thread of the work in Gestalt. Indeed, the concept of theme is central to the process of supporting a person's change from a Gestalt perspective. What I am about to share is a bit difficult to understand. Bear with it.

Here is a new definition to add to the one we have developed. *Theme is: uppermost figure plus direction.*

Remember that pastoral caring is concerned with the movement of people from one way of relating to the world and themselves to another. Whether it be in a pastoral visit, leading a meeting, or teaching a class, pastoral caring is concerned with helping a person or persons change and move from how they are living their life to a new way of living life. In Gestalt terms, they are aware of a "want or a need"–the new way of relating.

Let me supply some midpoint illustrations. Parents may desire to change how they parent; adults may desire to develop new ways of relating to aging parents; church committees may desire new ways of organizing. In each of these cases, there is an expressed need, or want to change. That is one-half of the uppermost figure: the desire to change. The other half of theme is: *The resistance to the want or need to change.* In other words, as much as I might like to change or to try on a new way of being, part of me desires to maintain the old way. The uppermost figure is comprised of: *The need/want and the resistance to the need and want.*

Congratulations, you now understand one-half of theme.

The second half is *direction*. Let me illustrate direction. Imagine you are in a football game and you are running toward the goal line. In front of you are the biggest tackles this side of anywhere. You stop. You need to go ahead and score the winning touchdown. Then again, that may not be a great idea considering the human wall that has taken up residence between you and the goal. So, you could run like crazy and try to score. You could back up, and get as far away from these people as possible. You could also move ten yards forward and ten yards back and experience that decision. So, direction is one of three things: (1) going with the want, the desired change; (2) going with the resistance, or persisting as you are; (3) going between the two, trying on some old and new.

Theme: organizes your work . . . sets direction . . . provides energy.

The concepts of "direction" and "theme" are central to applying gestalt principles to your ministry. Gestalt is principled upon awareness and choice. The concept of theme is the principle in action. By attending to the choice of direction fully, you support the movement toward change. You support the natural decision-making process, the tension, that exists within all of us: the tension of "Sure, I'd like to change. Then again, I'd like to stay the same. Then again, gee, I don't know which way to go."

By attending to the direction, you support the decision process. You can even transform the "I'm not sure which way to go" into "I'd like to try both sides."

What Do I Need To Be Aware of When I Am Developing Themes with People?

First, remember that themes need to be mutually agreed upon. Do not inflict your thematic idea upon another person. In the example I gave of the young woman setting relationship limits, we agreed upon the theme, and hence the potential direction of the work.

You might share an idea and explore it with the other in order to create a clear figure for work. However, since the theme becomes the focus of work, it is important that it be mutually understood and agreed upon. The theme needs to be supported with sufficient ground to be developed and explored for growth. If it is not explored fully, it may lack the energy and interest to be of value for the other. Remember that themes are a product of the figure/ground relationship as well. As such, they too must recede to ground after being figural. In other words, when a theme has lost its usefulness, allow another to develop.

Here Are Some Illustrations

I will keep these rather simple to make the point of how themes can be developed and utilized.

Imagine working with a father. He has a son in his early teens. The two have not been close, but the father would like to create some closeness. Through the course of the pastoral counseling session, several minithemes are noted: the man's own father was rather distant, the parishioner has recently turned 40 and wants to begin a new way of life with his family, and his son seems interested in knowing him.

The uppermost figure is comprised of the need: the father's desire to communicate more with his son. It also includes the resistance to this need/want: remaining, persisting as they are—distant.

The direction could be going with the need/want: exploring ways of creating more linkage with his son. He could also go with the resistance, and continue as he is, or even it do it some more. (This will become more understood after reading "The Paradoxical Theory of Change.") He could also do some of each: try out a new way, and try one the old style. Each way of working this theme would have a different outcome, each having been developed in support of increasing awareness and the uppermost figure.

Another example deals with a church meeting. There is a want/need to redefine how church meetings are run. Church meetings seem too dictatorial for some. There is a resistance to any change at all by others.

There is a problem here. Is the theme clear enough? Maybe not. So, more ground might be developed with final figure of desiring to encourage more lay leadership at meetings on all levels of church life.

The uppermost figure is the need/want to promote more lay involvement and the resistance is continuing with clergy leadership.

The possible directions: (1) go with the want and explore the meaning of the new lay leadership program for meetings; (2) go with the resistance and explore the meaning of continuing or even increasing the level of clergy leadership; (3) go with the polarity between the two and have some meetings with lay leadership, some with clergy leadership.

It Seems I Would Be Very Active in This Process

You are right. Gestalt allows and encourages utilizing your relationship and your experience as a participant in the process of change. That is one of the important reasons why I believe Gestalt fits so well with pastoral caring. Gestalt values the relationships that exist between persons as ingredients in the helping process.

A Final Note About Theme

Theme can be a difficult concept to master. Take some time to attend to the themes you face every day. Be aware of themes when you choose to do things differently, or the same as before. What happens when you feel caught in "the land of in-between" and need to explore and experience both the want to change as well as persist? The principle of theme can take hold and become usable by you the more you allow yourself to experience the themes in your life. Take a risk, and choose your directions—the old, the new, or something in the middle—and attend to your experience.

Some Ideas for Your Growth

Theme is something we experience every day, but are not always aware of at any given moment. To heighten your awareness of theme, choose a newspaper or magazine article. Read every other paragraph in reverse order. Notice any thread or theme? What happens to the theme? Has the figural theme lost its supportive ground? Has your understanding become confused?

Attend to movies, television, radio or stage productions. How clear are the themes? What happens when the theme is not clear? Does the meaning of the production become lost?

Finally, take a moment and reflect when you have been at a meeting where little was accomplished. Perhaps the goal and purpose of the meeting were not clear. How would the concept of theme have impacted the meeting?

NOTES

1. Gestalt Institute of Cleveland, postgraduate training program, year one.
2. Gestalt Institute of Cleveland, postgraduate training program, year one.
3. Gestalt Institute of Cleveland, postgraduate training program, year one.

Chapter 8

Contact Boundary and Self-Regulation

> In Gestalt therapy, the meeting of differences is called contact so, [the] meeting of the sand and sea is contact. The event thus created by this meeting of differences is called the contact boundary . . . The contact boundary takes into account both the differences between the elements which are meeting and also the unity of the meeting, the whole created by it.[1]

What Is "Contact Boundary" and How Does It Relate to the Practice of Gestalt Theory?

Key to Gestalt theory is the relationship that exists between organisms, between what is the organism and what is not the organism: the Known and the Unknown. It is at this point, the point where the "I and Thou" the "me and what is not me" meet, at the point of contact, that change occurs. This is the "contact boundary." This term of contact does not mean joining. Contact requires separation and a clear awareness (there's that word again) of who I am. Clear contact requires self-awareness and the risk of making contact, of being captured.

In the previous paragraph of this section, I mentioned change. It is important to understand that from a Gestalt view, change occurs both naturally and as a matter of choice. Change occurs as the result of contact at the contact boundary. The work, from a Gestalt frame of reference, is to make a choice around the direction of the change. We experience this boundary daily, even moment by moment. Contact occurs each time we wonder, "Do I want to do this or not?" It occurs each time you read a paragraph and you wonder, "Do I want to believe this or not?" The boundary becomes apparent as contact is felt. We may become aware of it by an increase in energy in various forms: anxiety, questions, interest, or a general awareness of energy. This energy occurs at the point of and as a result of contact at the contact boundary.

Let us walk through some examples of "contact boundary" in operation. Imagine that you introduce an idea for a new order of worship at a worship committee meeting. You can feel the energy rise as discussion takes place; believe it or not, even debate occurs. The discussion is around what is known, the present order of worship, and the unknown, the proposed order of worship. The energy concerns the interest, the conflict, and the potential exchange between the known and the unknown.

Imagine that a person is told he or she will need the help of family in recovering from an illness. Ideas may be shared such as, "No, I can take care of myself" or "No one is going to see me naked, especially my children!"

Contact boundary is the meeting place of the known and unknown. It is where energy is shared, and movement toward a new awareness occurs.

Contact occurs at the point where the man's or woman's understanding of his or her self encounters his/her understanding of needing help, or being seen naked.

The discussion, the change, takes place here—at the contact boundary, in the here and now.

SELF-REGULATION

Gestalt therapy theory further assumes that all persons who go to therapy have within themselves the energy and resources necessary for self-regulation to function successfully. . . . Regardless of clients' statements that may emphasis weakness, dependency, and lack of ability to manage their lives, the therapist must assume that there are latent self-regulatory mechanisms of health within each client. The wholeness of persons is not merely a convenient concept or a psychological perspective, it is the bedrock of Gestalt therapy.[2]

What Is "Self-Regulation"?

"Self-regulation" is the process by which a person, or group of persons, moderates the forces for change. It is a concept, as well as an activity. Self-regulation is vital for the organism to maintain its identity. Without the capacity to self-regulate, we would be unable to maintain any sense of self. In many respects, what we are about as pastoral carers is aiding people in gaining the capacity to self-regulate, to support their own process and desire for change and growth.

Are There Various Styles of Boundary Regulation?

There is a continuum of boundary contact styles of self-regulation. They range from extremely flexible, when, or perhaps where, change occurs rather easily. On the other end, there can be a rigid boundary style. Here, people present themselves as highly defensive regarding any sort of change. They may be fearful of change or the result of change. The boundary appears rigid and absolute.

In the practice of gestalt, enabling persons to become more aware of themselves aids in choosing the contact style appropriate for differing situations. In this manner, they may become more creative in how they "do" change, not always relying upon one "standard" style.

Contact boundary and self-regulation provide the edge to your work. It determines where and how intensely change will take place.

By having a fuller understanding of what is occurring at the point of contact, people become more able to regulate their process of understanding and change in a way that is respectful of themselves.

How Do the Concepts of "Rigid and Flexible Boundaries" Affect My Work?

On the continuum of contact styles, different internal processes are at work within people. The very fact that people appear rigid or flexible may speak to their ability to adapt and perhaps to their investment in what is being addressed.

Imagine that you are going to introduce an idea to a worship committee–choosing a new hymnal perhaps. You notice that the energy rises, and sides are taken to be defended. This boundary is *rigid*.

Your task may be to soften the contact boundary so ideas can be exchanged, or at least to identify the values at play in this boundary. The tools: figure/ground and process versus content.

What Are the Inherent Dangers in the Rigid Boundary?

Rigid boundaries inhibit "give," so change of any type, even a discussion of it, may prove difficult. They may also indicate a fear of loss of self, so little energy can be let out, and shared.

At the same time, the rigid boundaries may indicate a strong belief in a principle or ideal. Rigid boundaries, in and of themselves are not good or bad, they just are. The question is whether or not they are healthy to have at any given moment.

Imagine the worship meeting, and the topic of using a different colored ink on the church bulletin is raised for discussion. There will probably be less energy expended than in the hymnal discussion. Discussion may revolve more around logistics than the meaning of the change. This boundary is more flexible, and has more "give" to it.

Just as persons with a more rigid boundary appear to have a fear of loss of self, persons with more flexible boundaries lose themselves easily. These more flexible people may need to become more rigid, more clearly defined. The task for both is the same: become more aware of their contact style.

Boundary contact and self-regulation increase the awareness of the ground, support the figure of change, and provide the energy for the movement to change.

For both, the task is to aid in experiencing themselves more fully at the points of contact and potential change. In the hymnal question, this might mean noting the energy in the room, and then asking people what they find valuable in the present hymnal. In the case of the more flexible boundary, the bulletin ink question, the same might be true. You might ask about what appeals to them in the look of the bulletin. In both cases, you are increasing the ground so the figure, the decision, has more to stand upon.

Why Help the More Flexible People Become More Aware? After All, They Are Willing and Able to Change Already.

Are they really willing to change? Are they aware of themselves? This question seems to lean toward defining flexible boundaries as "better" than rigid. Attend to how you experience boundaries and the value judgments you may place upon them.

Let me answer this question in two parts. First, remember the goal is not to simply make people change. The goal is to help people become more aware of themselves, which will allow them to grow and either change or remain the same, with self-support.

There is value in heightening the awareness of persons who have, apparently, flexible boundaries. Sometimes these boundaries are not what they appear to be.

Someone, or even a group of people, may in fact demonstrate a true ease in changing by saying, "No problem, I'm flexible." However, when given the opportunity to speak of the personal feelings and values that they have in the change, their boundary may become more clearly defined and less flexible. They come to know themselves better. They may have an *introject* about being flexible. (Remember this term for later study.)

In many respects, contact styles are a learned behavior. The task is to enable yourselves and those you care for and with, to be more fully aware of themselves and their contact style. In this way you, and they, can be clearly aware of making "boundary contact" and regulate or choose the shape of change that may occur.

What Should I Keep in Mind When I Experience the Contact Boundary?

A key belief in gestalt is that of "safe emergencies." This concept is important since when you work toward change, you are working at the contact boundary. This boundary may be a well-known and familiar place for people; it may also be fear-filled.

When people make contact with the "known and unknown," they are vulnerable to themselves and others. It is important to be aware of their need to maintain a sense of self-identity amid these changing seas. Any process of change needs to be done in awareness on your part, as well as others. Each point of contact needs to be created in such as way that the contact boundary and its effect can be regulated and tolerated. The term is called "grading." It is the creation of a safe emergency. Let me share some examples.

You have just told some church members you are going to alter the worship service. There is a moment of silence, and then the energy rises in the room, as do the voices. People speak of the importance of tradition in worship and their fears of how people will adjust. In essence, the contact boundary was struck fully, the boundary became rigid, and people became anxious.

A way to grade the discussion could be to talk about the potential of modifying the worship service, or asking for feedback about the worship life of the church. In this way, contact between the known and unknown occurs with the potential to assimilate change, with a feeling of being safe in the midst of an emergency. Once again, the gestalt foundation concepts of figure ground—process versus content—come into play.

In counseling, the process of grading and self-regulation is just as important. By sensing the energy and comfort in the relationship, you can tell if you have, to use an old phrase, had people "bite off more than they could chew." The solution is simple: Make the pieces smaller.

To help another, you are responsible for developing the safe emergency to support the process of change. The creation of this safe emergency is critical for the development of trust and movement toward change.

Earlier, I mentioned the anxiety at the point of contact. This is a key barometer for Gestalt work. You need to support sufficient anxiety at the contact boundary to create energy for change. At the same time, you need to regulate the energy so the system does not become overloaded. Again, you are part of the system, and your awareness matters in this balancing act.

Inherent in understanding self-regulation is the gestalt view of "resistance." This will be explored more fully in the next section of this project.

Some Ideas for Your Growth

Take some time to explore how you "make contact" with the world outside yourself. In what situations do you experience yourself setting firmer boundaries than others? What do you experience that makes this style of boundary needed?

In your own faith, in what issues do you find yourself more or less flexible? What concerns do you find offer more "give" to other opinions?

In Scripture, what stories speak of contact boundary and self-regulation? Read the stories of the calling of the disciples. Who joined willingly? Who needed to pause?

What of Jesus' going of to the hills to pray? What models does Jesus provide for boundary contact and self-regulation?

NOTES

1. Joel Latner, "The Theory of Gestalt Therapy," in *Gestalt therapy: Perspectives and application*, edited by Edwin C. Nevis (New York: The Gestalt Institute of Cleveland Press, 1992), 25.

2. Margert P. Korb, Jeffrey Gorrell, and Vernon Van De Riet, *Gestalt therapy: Practice and theory* (Needham Heights, MA: Allyn and Bacon, 1989), 13.

Chapter 9

Polarities

Polarization occurs when an individual identifies strongly with one end of a set of opposite characteristics. In Gestalt therapy, it is understood that the polarization process leads frequently to misattributed self and self/other definitions with a tendency to invest more and more energy in maintaining the pole with which the person has identified. A further result of such polarizations is the subsequent denial of experiences or characteristics that do not conform to the person's existing constructs.[1]

What Are "Polarities"?

The concept of polarities is key to the gestalt understanding of change. A clear incorporation of this concept is key to supporting the process of change and growth. Simply, polarities involve the belief that when there is one feature you are exploring, there is always an opposing feature. In other words, whenever there is an "x," there exists the polarity of "x." In gestalt terms, you can go toward "x" or away from or against "x." To accent, or lean into one of the poles, you make clearer contact not only with the pole you are leaning into, but with the other as well. You may remember this concept from the "theme" section earlier.

How Is This Useful?

We all know the sense of powerlessness we feel at times. Frequently, we feel powerless to change the course of our lives, or to make decisions in general. I have found that these feelings of powerlessness stem from a lack of awareness of polarities. People become frozen in one place, with little or no awareness of where they stand.

When people have the capacity and opportunity to explore their polarities, their choices increase. They are able to integrate where they are, and where they are not. This can increase their sense of personal ground and support the development of fuller figures.

How Is the Concept Utilized in Pastoral Caring?

I utilize it in many aspects of pastoral caring. In a very simple way, I ask people who feel stuck in one behavior how they would act if they did not act in that fashion. Sounds simple, doesn't it? As people apply the concept of polarities in their lives, they become aware of their potential for and resistances toward change.

I remember working with a couple who communicated primarily through fighting. I think we have all known people like this. They came into session wanting to talk about the recent fight and to decide who was right and who was wrong. They wanted to work on the "content" of the fight, and not the "process" of their communication.

I asked them to attend to the polarity of their focus on fighting, asking "What would it be like to not fight?" A simple question? No, not really. It was new to them. They began to discuss the other side of the polarity, and had great difficulty in describing it. As you can imagine, it was a great journey for them to learn of options they had before them, but had never been aware of. Working in the here and now, they addressed how they were, and how they were not. They were given the support needed to explore a new opportunity

---

Polarities offer the opportunity to explore the other, less natural, less well-known parts of ourselves. Exploration of polarities can widen and deepen understanding and awareness.

I experience polarities at work frequently in the realm of committee work. Here, people feel stuck in certain ways of leading, or participating in meetings. In these cases, I might ask them to discuss what the polarity of leadership might be, "What would it be like if we worked like (x) instead of (y)?" I then ask them to behave "as if" this was occurring in the here and now.

I have found that working "as if" becomes a playful learning experience for people. They have a chance to try on a new behavior, or way of acting, without the threat of failure. After it is all over, they not only know more about the new behavior, but the "old" one as well. It is fun.

In general, I utilize the concept of polarities by stating, "I'm curious about the other side. I wonder what it would be like for you if you did (the opposite)." In this rather simple statement, people become aware of both where they are and where they are not. Choices then become possible.

Some Ideas for Your Growth

It is important to gain an awareness of your polarities. So, take a moment and bring to your mind something you believe, or believe in right now. Now, right now, what do you experience? Do you experience comfort, or silence? Do you experience a sense of peace? Now, take a moment and imagine the polarity of that experience. What do you experience now? Do you feel less peaceful and quiet? How does your increased awareness of the polarity increase your awareness of each?

NOTE

1. Margaret P. Korb, Jeffrey Gorrell, and Vernon Van De Riet, *Gestalt therapy: Practice and theory* (Needham Heights, MA: Allyn and Bacon, 1989), 14.

Chapter 10

Resistance

Traditionally, resistance implies that a person has specific goals which can be identified, like visiting a friend, doing homework, or writing a song. Any intrapersonal interference to moving in these directions is called a resistance, a stubborn barrier, alien to the person's natural behavior. The barrier must be removed, according to this view, so that the "right" goal may be reached.[1]

Instead of seeking to remove the resistance, it is better to focus on it assuming that, at best, a person grows through resisting and, at worst, the resistance is nevertheless a part of his identity.[2]

Creative adjustment replaces the conventional term "resistance" in the vocabulary of Gestalt therapy. Resistance is the usual psychological characterization for the individual's seeming unwillingness to change or grow, or to accept the therapist direction. . . . But resistance is creative adjustment and organismic self-regulation. It is integral to the person's "being" in the world, and no approach driving at holistic solutions can ask a person to set aside parts of themselves.[3]

Resistance is a term that connotes an external observation of my state of reluctance. . . . And what appears to you, on your observing surface, as a casual reluctance to change my be an inner crisis for me, a fight for my life. This is the phenomenological definition of resistance, a definition which stresses the validity of my inner experience, my inner life.[4]

What Is the Gestalt View of Resistance, and How Does It Compare to the Traditional Views?

There is a great difference between the more traditional views of resistance and the gestalt view. The gestalt view has a difference not only in theory, but in practice. To discuss the gestalt view, some background might be helpful.

In the early days of psychoanalysis, resistance was viewed as a defense. It was viewed as something that interfered with the progress of therapy. It was "bad." Freud said that the goal of psychotherapy was to bring the unconscious material of the client from the past into the present. He contended that "resistance" was the client's inability to do this. This inability was to be overcome and fought against.

Wilheim Reich understood resistance as being presented through the muscular process. He believed that tight muscles were signs of withheld emotions. He believed that these emotions were unavailable to the client and needed to be surfaced.

Fritz Perls, the creator of Gestalt therapy, felt that Reich was on the right track. Perls shared the body/mind connection that Reich promoted. However, Reich felt too that the physical process interfered with the "true self" in therapy. Resistance, as with Freud, was seen as "bad" and getting rid of it was seen as "good." Indeed, this ridding of resistance was the goal of therapy.[5]

So, What Is the Gestalt View?

Resistances are, simply, creative ways of saying "no." Gestalt views resistance as an important and necessary part of a person. It is how the person "self-regulates" and remains safe. Resistance belongs to and is a necessary part of a person, or systems ability to feel and remain whole during the process of change.

We will discuss specific resistances in the second section of this text. Remember that resistances, the apparent inability for a person or system to change, is not bad, nor is it good. It simply is.

For a moment, imagine jumping off a bridge while tied to a bungee cord. Really. Take a moment and imagine it. First you walk up to the takeoff point. Then, the harness is strapped on and you walk to the edge and *jump*. Well, maybe you jump. Maybe you pause. Maybe you cross yourself, or say a quick prayer. Maybe you do just jump. The pausing is simply a way to say, "No, not right now." These are resistances.

So, Resistances Are To Be Appreciated, Not Fought Against?

Yes. Resistances have value, and this value needs to be explored and appreciated and utilized. The following story illustrates this. I was working with a couple, and for some reason, I felt anxious with them. No reason why, I just knew my stomach was more tense than usual and I sensed I was more vigilant than usual. Within a few minutes, I knew why. The husband debated every statement I made. He would always find the exception, and tell me. I found myself getting angry, feeling like I was in a judo match trying to outwit him. In fact, I did try to outwit him. Needless to say, this first session bombed.

After some supervision over my outwitting attempt, I decided to not fight his resistance at the next session. I chose to give him some space to explore his ideas and even began to incorporate his ideas into the session. I stopped fighting his resistance, allowing his feelings and ideas to become "figural" instead of our theoretical arm wrestling. By increasing his awareness of his own ideas, he was able to see their limitations as well their potentials. In fact, we were both more able to be in the moment.

What became clear was his fear of being "bullied" by someone else. His resistance was a creative way of saying, "Wait, I have some ideas too. I can't simply give up my ideas and take on yours."

Now, for an experiment. This takes two people, so read and then go find someone with whom to try it out.

First, stand a few feet apart from your partner with your feet apart. Now, each of you put your arms in front of yourself. Without moving your feet, and pushing only with your hands, try to push the other person over. What happens?

Usually, people try to push hard. Then they learn: the harder you push, the more *you* are controlled by the other person. In effect, you give the other person your energy. The trick: put enough pressure to "make contact" with the other person, but not so much as to fight the person. You will find that if you just make contact, you can move the other's hands wherever you desire.

Try other styles too. What happens when you let pressure off one hand and not the other? What happens if you lower your arms or raise them above shoulder height? What happens when you resist "hard" or "softly?"

This is also a good experiment for figure/ground understanding. Experiment with how close your feet are front to back and side to side. Notice what happens if you do not have enough "ground" for your "figure." Check it out.

So, What Is the Goal of "Working with Resistances?"

The goal is the core goal of gestalt—aiding the person in becoming aware experientially of his or her resistances. The key element here is that in becoming aware of when and how he or she resists, or blocks the change process, each is able to choose whether or not to continue the behavior. One is able to make *choices* in one's actions.

Why Is Knowing How We Resist Important?

It can be important in several ways. First, if we bring resistance to awareness, we can explore it—make it figural—and learn about ourselves through it. What value does the resistance have? How does it help or harm us?

As a person becomes aware of the resistance, he or she is able to, in a fashion, walk around and examine the resistance. Sometimes she or he can move right on by it. Sometimes this is not possible, and she or he may have to spend time getting to know the resistance better and choose when to move beyond it. Each grows to appreciate and sometimes learn of the valuable role these resistances have played in daily living. Resistances are invisible and out of our awareness—until we get close to them.

In understanding our resistances, we can come to appreciate their value and place in our lives. Then, and only then, we can truly choose to remain with the resistance, or resist it and continue with the change process.

When Do People Become Aware of Their Resistances?

Resistances are much like heat. You do not always know it is there, but as you come closer to it, there is no mistaking it. Remember I mentioned that resistances are creative ways of saying no? We are aware of our resistances when we experiences ourselves pausing and saying, in effect, "No, not yet." The closer we come to the resistance, the more pronounced the resistance will become. We become aware of its presence and power. The goal is to become aware of the value and place of the resistance.

So, resistances are not the enemy to be feared or hated. In some respects, resistances are misunderstood friends, and need to be appreciated. Think about it for a moment. These resistances, these creative ways of saying no, have kept the person out of harm's way for some time. Resistances have a place in life. There is never a time to "tear them down."

But This Goes Against the Idea of "Get a Grip and Move on" That Many People Promote

Thankfully, it does. To tell someone to "get a grip" is not to appreciate the struggle they live with, and devalues the person. Getting a grip does not take into account the story of the person or the value of the resistance.

I always remember: At any given moment, a person is always doing the best he or she absolutely can—at that moment. This means that at any moment, all of us are facing life as fully as we can and any resistances that might be in the equation need to be there. Our task is to help people become aware of their resistances and choose to keep, lose, or change them. There are so many factors, including resistances and beyond, that exert control over our abilities at any moment.

Resistance is not to be fought against, wrestled with, or in any manner combatted; it is to be admired as a creative way of saying, "No, not right now . . . I'm not ready." By bringing the resistance to awareness, you develop still more ground to support the figure.

Can You Illustrate Dealing with Resistances?

I can, but I will wait until the next section. Now, there is a resistance. In the section, "The Gestalt Cycle of Experience," the "undoing" of resistances will become more clear.

Some Ideas for Your Growth

Resistance is a part of each of us. No matter how laid back and "go with the flow" we may appear, we all resist. The task is to become aware of our styles of resistance.

So, someday as you are driving down the street, stick your hand out your window. (Make sure people do not think you are making a left turn.) Now, pivot your hand like a wing. Pay attention to how resistance changes as you place more and more area against the force of the wind.

Next, with someone you know and trust, try this experiment: Have the person ask you to do something simple such as tying your shoes. Now, try saying no with various styles of speech. What is it like? When does the resistance fit the request, and what do you experience when you go past that point?

Finally, how do you resist? Do you resist with your voice, your body language, or perhaps all of yourself? How have people resisted in Scripture? How do they creatively say "no?"

NOTES

1. Erving Polster and Miriam Polster, *Gestalt therapy integrated: Contours of theory and practice* (New York: Vintage Books, 1974), 51-52.

2. Polster and Polster, 68.

3. Joel Latner, "The Theory of Gestalt Therapy," in *Gestalt theory: Perspectives and applications,* edited by Edwin C. Nevis (New York: The Gestalt Institute of Cleveland Press, 1992), 28.

4. Joseph Zinker, *Creative process in gestalt therapy* (New York: Vintage Books, 1978), 121.

5. Elaine Kepner, Lecture notes, Gestalt Institute of Cleveland, February 1991.

Chapter 11

Confluence

This mechanism, as with Perls, is an overidentification of self with the environment, a failure to perceive and distinguish the *boundary* between the two, by which the organism identifies and knows itself. Thus, excitement, the energy at the boundary for the contact resolution, is diffused and unlocalized, not brought to bear on the problem as aggressive energy for a new solution.[1]

When we are in the state of confluence, we do not experience ourselves as being distinct from our environment; we merge into the beliefs, attitudes and feelings that surround us (Swanson, 1988). We feel safe in our confluence with our families, our jobs, or our professions, but our own personal experience is denied. Contact with the environment, established through clear awareness of self and not-self is minimal. Through projection, introjection, retroflection, and deflection, the boundaries between the individual and the environment are confused and distorted. Through confluence, awareness of boundaries is seriously impaired.[2]

What Is "Confluence"?

If resistance is the pushing against the flow of change, then confluence is the opposite. Confluence is going so much with the flow that there is no resistance. There is no resistance, no shift in the flow, no differentiation between who I am and who I am not.

There is a scene in the movie, *The Hunt for Red October* where the U.S. submarine is following the Soviet submarine. The command is given for the U.S. sub to mirror every move of the other. In this way, they are told, the Soviets will be unaware of them. The U.S. sub was acting in a confluent manner. It was making no move that would be distinctive for it. Its direction and action was dictated by the other.

Does Someone Act in Either a Confluent or Nonconfluent Manner? Is It an Either/Or Proposition?

Not, not really. Imagine a road. On one end of the road is the little town of "Isolation." On the other end of the road is the town of "Completely Merging." Isolation has a sentry guard on the edge of town. Nothing gets in or out of this town. Meanwhile, at Completely Merging, there are no guards. As a matter of fact, no one there ever asks a question about what goes in or out.

This road is the continuum of confluence. If a boundary is highly rigid, or highly resistant, there is no confluence. You know the boundary. There is a clear distinction between parties.

On the other end, if a boundary has no resistance, no edge, it creates the condition of confluence. There is a complete merging of the parties. The distinct identity of each is lost in the identity of the other.

How Does This Present Itself in My Work?

As pastoral carers, we are trained to be caring and supportive. Hopefully we begin our studies with this attitude. Sometimes we may get the idea that to be caring and supportive means to always say yes, always agree, and never cause friction. It is as if our "M.O." or goal is to always support, and never challenge. All of these are ways that we become confluent.

Confluence does not support the difference between "I" and "Thou." There is no barrier between the two. In essence, both parties become invisible, unaware of themselves or of each other.

I have found that when confluence is lived out, it is frequently perceived as tacit agreement. If others do not experience any difference from you, they assume you agree with and support their position.

Early in my ministry, I served a yoked parish. I was associate pastor of a congregation of 750 and pastor of a congregation of 100. My first day there, I was told there was going to be a dinner to celebrate the start of my ministry. It had been agreed that the smaller congregation could send a limited number of persons, while the larger church's entire congregation would be invited.

I sat there, and nearly agreed. I did agree with the idea of a celebration. I like dinners. I could not "go along with," or be confluent, with the unequal invitations. Although it was difficult for me to do, I felt it was important that I be experienced as having my own ideas. I did not agree with them, and I stated that, "All, or only the leadership from both—or no one at all." To have been confluent would have been to go along with the decision. After all, I was new and had just been ordained. What right did I have to question?

Confluence can occur easily and without intent in pastoral caring situations. As I said, we are taught to be kind. We are confluent when we simply agree and do not, even for a moment, resist the seemingly natural flow of things. We are confluent when we do not nudge parents just into developing two ways of discipline, instead of the one they know. Without the resistance, we are saying we agree. We are confluent when we accept a tradition of leadership that does not allow for full participation. Our confluent style is perceived as agreement, and even the church's support, when we do not question moral issues of the day.

How Do I Know When Confluence Occurs?

Personally, I monitor my own sense of the flow of the work. Is it simply moving along, without any modifications occurring? Are questions being asked? Are people agreeing quickly to accept another position as their own? Am I feeling like people have a case of terminal niceness? If the process seems to be "too nice," I perceive it as confluent. The question is, do I choose to support the confluent nature of the work or not?

What Do I Do?

As usual, try to increase the awareness of the confluence. I have several methods that I use. In a meeting where people are agreeing quickly with little discussion, I will slow the process down. I will ask them for more details so more ground has an opportunity to be developed. This process provides the ground for people to disagree, modify the figure, and at least agree by choice. In this way, the figure, the decision, allows more choices to be made.

In a counseling setting, I sense confluence when people agree quickly, or say, "You're right" without missing a beat. I tell people, "I have a little rule here. No one can answer a question less than three seconds after the question is asked. So, take a long breath before you answer." This too provides ground for a shift of figures from confluence, with no individual identity, to more distinct identity of each party.

So, Confluence Is To Be Avoided

Not so much avoided as to be mindful of it. There is a great distance between being a citizen of the little town of Isolation or the town of Completely Merging.

Confluence is simply another contact style. The difference is that in this contact style, there is less distinction between persons. Sometimes confluence may be needed; for example, when ideas are simply being asked for. Other times, it may be detrimental to the process. The task is, as you know by now, to become aware of and make choices about confluence.

Some Ideas for Your Growth

Next time you are in a gathering of people, pay attention to the confluent/nonconfluent features of the conversation. Attend to the energy flow and focus of the conversation. What do you notice?

Confluence can be part of the process of change if it is attended to and brought into awareness. What does it mean when someone chooses to become invisible, enveloped by another?

If you are involved in a counseling experience, pay attention to your confluent style. What are your barometers for being confluent?

How "in touch" with yourself or the process are you when you are more or less confluent?

Finally, pay attention to where you are confluent in life. Is it by choice, or by established pattern?

NOTES

1. Gordon Wheeler, *Gestalt reconsidered: A new approach to contact and resistance* (New York: The Gestalt Institute Press, 1991), 78.

2. Margaret P. Korb, Jeffrey Gorrell, and Vernon Van De Riet, *Gestalt therapy: Theory and practice* (Needham Heights, MA: Allyn and Bacon, 1989), 60.

Chapter 12

The Paradoxical Theory of Change

Change is paradoxical in the Gestalt approach . . . If a person is constantly trying to improve, that person is focusing on a gestalt about "trying" that will never be finished. That person changes only by stopping the attempts at improvement and by allowing him or herself to be exactly what he or she is, thus opening the way to confront unfinished gestalten. The only way unfinished gestalten may be completed is by affirming the truth, no matter what it is. . . . Persons can only be what they are. When they are totally in the present, they do not have a sense of change and yet, they are changing.[1]

What Is the "Paradoxical Theory of Change"?

Usually, when we think of change or someone changing, we assume that people need to change or move to the new direction or belief they want. From the Gestalt perspective, that is not true. Frances Harris from the Gestalt Institute of Cleveland wrote:

Gestalt theory and method has a particular philosophical base than may be different that your initial reaction (to a previous assignment). It is the foundation for everything that we do. Beisser (1970) has articulated what is the very essence of Perls' work which he calls "The Paradoxical Theory of Change" . . . that change occurs when one becomes what he is, and not when he tries to be what he is not "when the patient abandons, or at least for the that moment, what he would like to become and attempts to become what he is. Change does not take place through a coercive attempt by the individual or another person to change him, but it does take place if one is

79

willing to take the time and effort to be what he is . . . to be fully invested in his current position."[2]

The paradox is that to change, we must accept and embrace that *which is* and not simply that which is yet to become. We need to invest time and energy in knowing who we are in the moment not only the way we would like to be. I know it sounds fully backwards, but it is not. Simply stated, in order to change, we must pay attention to what it means to be the same.

To borrow from Fran Harris, choose a part of your personal style that you really do not like. Perhaps you do not like your shyness, your anger, your fear. Now, imagine yourself being even more of it. Yes, even more shy, or more angry, or more fear-filled.

What Does It All Prove?

It does not so much prove something as provide a unique way of understanding change. It is unique in that it values the "starting place" as much as the destination.

How Does It Work?

I once worked with a man whose voice caused him difficulty. Specifically, it was loud–very loud–all the time. To him, however, it was not loud–it was just his voice. For the rest of us in the Western hemisphere, it was loud.

Early in our work, he became aware of the effect of his voice on others. Let me say, he gained the knowledge of its effect. However, he was still unable to sense his voice as being loud. He still wanted to make his voice less loud, and more appealing–even though he did not fully understand the problem.

The work involved his voice becoming softer, right? No, not really. My first goal was that he would become more aware of his voice so that he would be able to choose how he wanted to use it.

The experiment was, as you might have predicted, to become aware of his voice as it was in the present. I wanted him to gradually gain an appreciation, an awareness, of his voice. First, I asked him to speak with the voice he usually presents. Then, I asked him to accent these qualities. Make the deep even deeper. Make the loud louder—but not so loud as to injure his voice. Make the staccato even sharper.

Then, without thought, he began to play with his voice. He tried on different volumes, tones, and tonal qualities. He even decided to try on the soft voice of a baby. The more he played, the more surprised he appeared. He learned to enjoy his voice.

In the end, he did indeed develop a softer voice. But he did it not by accenting his desired change to more softness, but rather in appreciating the "what was" of his voice: its strength. In this way, softness became the figure, based upon the ground of his existing voice.

The paradoxical theory of change was experienced—he did not fight for change. He lived in the moment, and change followed.

Change can occur by accepting and accenting sameness. By becoming more aware of what is, even if there is sameness, change can continue to be supported.

Some Ideas for Your Growth

The paradoxical theory of change is one of the most difficult for many to grasp in their study of Gestalt. So, take some time in the course of the day, and attend to changing something. It could be anything—the way you park your car, the ritual you have when you first sit at your desk. Think of some part of it you would like to change. Become aware of what *is* before you work toward what it is not. Then begin to try the change. How did your increased awareness of what was support you in this change?

Pause for a moment, and think back to a time when you wanted to change something about yourself, and felt powerless. What are you experiencing now? Pay attention to your experience. What does it say to you? Can you give your feeling a voice?

NOTES

1. Margaret P. Korb, Jeffrey Gorrell, and Vernon Van De Riet, *Gestalt therapy: Practice and theory* (Needham Heights, MA: Allyn and Bacon, 1989), 70.
2. Gestalt Institute of Cleveland, postgraduate training program, year one.

Chapter 13

Level of Systems

Gestalt and group dynamics theories draw from general systems theory the notion of "system openness," and share the assumption that system functioning is optimized by boundaries that are intact and definable, yet pliable and semipermeable. . . . In the context of gestalt theory, the development of the contact boundary allows for the injection of that which is assimilable, and the rejection of that which is inassimilable. In the context of group dynamics, semipermeable boundaries allow for a greater "database" for expanded choice and consensual validation.[1]

Can You Supply a Quick Definition of "Systems Theory"?

Systems theory states that in a relationship, all participants are linked together. This linkage creates two working principles:

1. Each set of relationships has a predictable pattern of relating. This pattern will continue undisturbed and unchanged until a change occurs to any member of the relationship.
2. A system strives for homeostatic balance. In this way, a system which has been "bumped" into a new style of relating will naturally attempt to rebalance itself into the previous state.

Systems theory is also called the principle of "Circular Causality" which differs from linear causality. Linear causality understands change as occurring in a straight line—cause leads to effect and there is no established relationship between the elements of the system.

Another application from "Circular Causality" and systems theory is how change can occur. Visualize a circle, with elements of the relationship at the north, south, east, and west points. The circle is spinning, with each element being effected and effecting others. In theory, you can effect change in this system of relationships by affecting *any* of the elements. So, you can effect change in many ways from a great variety of places in the relationship.

Several years ago I was in training at a local family therapy center. A family came in for a session: mom, dad, and "the kid." The son had been calling his mother at work each day, asking her to bring him home from school since he was feeling ill. As usually happens, the parents viewed the child as the one to be treated in therapy.

As we spoke to the family, we found out that the mother/wife had recently returned to the workforce. As a group, we wondered if perhaps this child was trying to rebalance the family relationship–stabilize the circle. Sure enough, as the family spoke of the changes in their lives, the son spoke up, "See Dad, I got Mom home just like you wanted."

Our directions to the family were aimed at the son: "Next time you feel sick, call your father." The father nearly leapt from his chair, "What? I have to work . . . ", to which the mother replied, "Well, what do you think I'm doing?"

In this example, the son worked to rebalance the system by having his mother come home. As a staff, we redirected the energy of the family from "fixing the kid" to working on their own system definition and redefining themselves as a family with two working parents. We intervened by making figural not the child, but the relationship between the parents and their expectations. As a staff, we shifted the son from being figural, as he was for his parents, to ground.

By the way, the child ceased to be sick at school after this session. Isn't counseling wonderful?

Does Gestalt Have Application Only with Individuals and Small Groups, or Can It Be Utilized Across Different Levels of Systems?

Gestalt, from the outset, views life from a perspective of wholeness. It is rather unique in that fashion within schools of psychology. It might be helpful to first define a few terms.

A system is, according to Dorothy Simonovich,

> . . . a bounded set of interrelated components and activities
> that constitute a single entity. This set of components work
> together for the overall objectives of the whole.[2]

I remember seeing a television show about 17 years ago about
various views of Chicago which provided a grand example of systems. The movie began with an aerial view of a home on the loop.
Gradually, the perspective shifted, and views were given from higher
and higher altitudes. It provided a view of the levels of system.

The first level was the home itself. Next was the street, and then
the neighborhood. The next level was the city, the county, and then
the state. The view of the systems continued to expand until it
included the region of the country, and the country itself. The levels
continued to expand until they included the hemisphere, the earth
itself, and finally, a view of the Milky Way from space.

Another example could be as simple as the arrangement of
grades in a school. One level of system is the school itself. The next
might be the grades, and the next the classes. It could further be
broken down by any number of defining characteristics.

So, How Does This Apply to Me in My Ministry?

It is vital to your application of gestalt to your work. Remember,
gestalt values the relationship that exists between people—that
includes you, and the people you care for. Too often, I fear, pastoral
care education classes do not stress enough the unique and powerful
relationship that exists between pastoral carers and those who
receive their care.

You are a system of one. When you are providing pastoral care
for another, you become a member of a two-person system. If you
are in a family setting, add to that system their children and you
have one system bound by the family, another defined by yourself
and the parents, another by yourself and the children, and still
another by the whole group.

From a gestalt perspective, the system we are a part of begins at
the atomic level; and moves to the universe. From a gestalt perspective, all of life is interrelated. Each is related to the other and is
responsible, in part, to and for the others.

From a gestalt view, you need to be constantly aware of what system you are participating in and affecting. This awareness can guide the quality and style of your attending, as well as being clearly aware of the figures to be developed.

How Does This Idea Impact My Work?

What I feel that it does for me is to help define my work. If you can take in the idea that when you are caring for another, the two of you are a bound system, you claim your participation with that person and with the energy in the space you share.

I have found that unless I clearly understand the level of systems I am part of, I cannot attend to myself, or to them. Frequently, the act of noting to all the level of systems being talked about allows for stalled work to proceed.

Level of systems understanding is also important in taking in as well as understanding the impact of any change in relationships. If we keep a systems perspective, we are more able to appreciate the impact, system wide, of an illness, a birth, a death, or any change.

All of the concepts discussed as well as those to be discussed later, can be applied to all levels of system. Committees, families, and other defined systems need to pay attention to figure/ground concepts when doing their work. At the same time, you can attend to the process and content work with various levels.

This too is one unique feature of gestalt work—it is applicable to any level of system, not simply a system called one person. The concepts of figure/ground, process versus content, and all the others can be utilized in understanding and working with yourself, as a system of one, or any number of other systems and relationships.

For me, the concept of levels of systems increases my awareness of the Holy Ground of life. With each system I am part of, I am also in relationship. Whether that system be family, work, city, state, country, environment, universe, or more, the relationship becomes holy.

Some Ideas for Your Growth

Levels of system and systems theory can be confusing concepts to master. Take some time to increase your awareness of the systems and levels of systems you are part of in everyday life.

Think of your home. How many systems are you part of at any one time? You have many different roles and identities. In some systems, you may indeed be at the center. In other systems you may be on the perimeter.

Take a moment. What are the connections that exist in your home? How does a change in one person affect all the people? Think of your work. What effect would your simply being a few minutes late have on the system? Think of your congregation. How would the departure of one family affect the whole body? We are all part of many unique systems, and Gestalt can be applied to all levels. Take the time and be aware.

NOTES

1. Mary Ann Huckabay, "An Overview of the Theory and Practice of Gestalt Group Process," in *Gestalt therapy: Perspectives and applications,* edited by Edwin C. Nevis (New York: The Gestalt Institute of Cleveland Press, 1992), 317.

2. Gestalt Institute of Cleveland, postgraduate training program, year two.

Chapter 14

Experiments

The experiment is the cornerstone of experiential learning. It transforms talking about into doing, stale reminiscing and theorizing into being fully here with all one's imagination, energy, and excitement. For example, by acting out an old, unfinished situation, the client is able to comprehend it in its richest context and to complete the experience using the resources of his present wisdom and understanding of life.[1]

What About the "Gestalt Experiments" I Hear So Much About? What Is Their Place in My Use of Gestalt?

As I said earlier, when people are asked what they know about Gestalt, they usually mention the experiments. They mention the use of "empty chairs" or having someone exaggerate their voice, or some physical action. They may even know about giving voice to tears, or to someone's body.

What they tend *not* to know about is the "why," or theory that supports the use or construction of the actual experiments. They may go to workshops to learn about the types, but they never take the time to learn about Gestalt itself. In truth, they have a figure, but very little ground.

What Are the Purposes of Gestalt Experiments?

The purpose of Gestalt experiments is to heighten the awareness of the person in the moment, in the here and now. The goal of the experiment is to remove the "aboutist deadlock," a deadlock caused by working from incomplete figure/ground, utilizing the tension within the person, real and able to be used for growth.

The Polsters wrote:

> The experiment in Gestalt therapy is an attempt to counter the aboutist deadlock by bringing the individual's action system right into the room. Through the experiment, the individual is mobilized to confront the emergencies of his life by playing out his aborted feelings and actions own relative safety. A safe emergency is thus created where venturesome exploration can be supported. Furthermore, both ends of the safety-to-emergency continuum can be explored, emphasizing first the support and then the risk taking, whichever seems salient at the time.[2]

What Is Meant by the "Safe Emergency"?

Think back to challenges you have faced. Perhaps your first sermon, your first wedding, your first skydive, or even your first date. Remember the tension and the anxiety. In a way, you were in the midst of an emergency.

Since in gestalt experiments we are joining people as they explore uncharted or unknown parts of themselves, the people are also in an emergency. Your task is to create a "safe emergency" where they are supported as they explore, engage, and move out of the change.

In the work of experiments, or any change work, your role is that of mentor and companion. Your role is to make certain sufficient ground has been developed so that a piece of work can be done. Your role is to aid in creating the environment for the experience and the experiment.

What Are the Principles of Experiments?

There are several:

1. We learn by doing.
2. We create safety so that risks can be taken.
3. We place the experiment at the boundary, in the midst of the tension between the want and the resistance.
4. Experiments occur in the present.
5. They are theme-based.

6. They always begin with the person respecting the integrity of the client's language.
7. They are graded up or down to support the development of a manageable and "integratable" piece of work.[3]

It Seems as if These Principles Would Make Sense in Any Gestalt Work, Not Just in Experiments.

You are right. They work across the realm of Gestalt. If you substitute the word "change" for experiment, you can apply these rules to your overall application of Gestalt. For example, "Change occurs at the boundary," "Change occurs in the present," or "Change is always theme-based."

What's So Special About Gestalt Experiments? Why Won't You Talk About Them More?

The experiment design is rather simple. The variety of experiment styles are not difficult to learn. However, using them properly and safely takes time to learn. It requires more ground than is possible in this short introduction. The experiments can create powerful experiences in both the creator of the experiment and the person involved in the experiment.

In many ways, experiments are like guns. They are simple to operate. However, when the person does not have sufficient training, experience, or respect for the gun, dangerous things can happen.

During the spring of my second year of training, I was with my Personal Growth Group that met four hours each weekend. We were a group of ten participants in the same year of our postgraduate training at the Gestalt Institute of Cleveland. For the past several sessions, I had been rather quiet.

For the previous few weeks, I had become aware of my lack of feelings. It seemed that dreadful things could happen around me, but I did not seem to feel anything. So, I shared my experience with the group. One of our leaders asked if I was interested in doing some work concerning this topic, and I agreed.

Together, we explored the issue more—in the here and now. He noted that my breathing was very shallow as I spoke, and I was bent over a bit. I was encouraged to pay attention to it. I noted that as I was more aware, I felt almost suffocated.

Together, we upgraded the experiment a bit. I sat in a straight-back chair with my facilitator kneeling behind me and to my right. He asked if he could put one hand on my back, and another on my chest. I agreed. The hand on my back was no problem, but when he touched my upper chest, I panicked. I literally stood up out of the chair and began to tremble.

I told him I did not know what happened, only that I was frightened. We spent some time getting regrounded, and then he placed his hand on a place that I identified as being safer, and began to compress my chest against my back. My job was to try to breathe. The harder I breathed, the harder he pushed.

Finally, I began to sob. My feelings of suffocation had been accented. I sobbed for the suffocation of my feelings, the lack of life I experienced. I cried for the feelings I had not let myself experience or express. The words came out painfully slow. I had become aware of my pain through the accenting of it.

To bring you into the moment as I write, I am crying. The memory of the power of the experience and the closeness I felt to my facilitator still lives in me.

---

*Experiments are **collaborative** in their development. They are not inflicted by the carer upon the other. As gestalt calls to understand the whole, so experiments must be developed **with** the other and **for** the other.*

Some Ideas for Your Growth

There is an endless supply of experiments. Creativity is the key. Here are two that you might try on your own. Hopefully, they will encourage you to learn more about Gestalt, and the power in the moment.

Next time you experience yourself being worried, give a voice to the part of your body in which you experience your worry. What would this part of your body say about feeling worried? Next time you find yourself tapping your foot, tap it even harder, and track your experience.

As you can see, experiments focus the energy of our work and move us ahead. They are wonderful when they work well . . . and dreadful when they do not.

NOTES

1. Joseph Zinker, *Creative process in gestalt therapy* (New York: Vintage Press, 1978), 123.

2. Erving Polster and Miriam Polster, *Gestalt therapy integrated* (New York: Vintage Books, 1973), 234.

3. Gestalt Institute of Cleveland, postgraduate training program, year one.

PART II:
THE GESTALT CYCLE
OF EXPERIENCE

Chapter 15

The Cycle of Experience

What Is the "Cycle of Experience"?

The Cycle of Experience is: . . . a description of forming and
completing figure, a description of organismic self-regulation.
It describes how we organize an experience and the ingredients.[1]

The cycle itself was developed at the Gestalt Institute of Cleveland. There, they adapted Perls' "metabolism cycle" and created
what is now known as the Gestalt Cycle of Experience.[2]

For our purposes, the Cycle of Experience offers a model for
following the process of change within any organism. It is a model
that, as you will see, provides a consistent framework to understand
the process and impediments of change.

The cycle consists of phases. Each phase has a specific role in the
movement toward change. These phases are: Sensation/Awareness,
Energy or Excitement, Action, Contact, and Assimilation and Withdrawal (see Figure 15.1). The Cycle of Experience also has resistances to it (see Figure 15.2).

Can You Give an Example of the Cycle in Operation?

The cycle occurs each moment of our lives. As adults, we are
unaware of the cycle itself or its phases. Infants, you may notice,
seem surprised by each new experience. They are aware of the cycle
through each experience. They are aware due to the newness of
each event.

You are reading one afternoon by the sunlight through your den
window. As the day draws on, you *sense* some tension behind your

FIGURE 15.1. The Gestalt Cycle of Experience

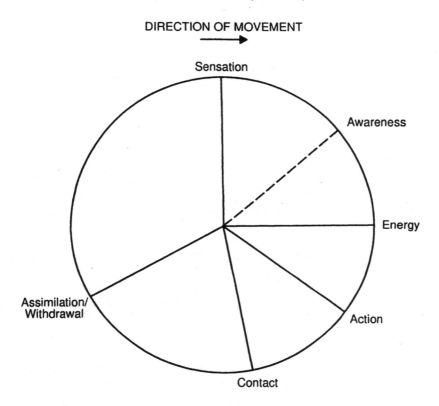

DIRECTION OF MOVEMENT

Sensation

Awareness

Energy

Assimilation/
Withdrawal

Action

Contact

Note: The proportion of each phase to the entire cycle of experience in the diagram does not represent the actual expenditure of time or energy. These properties will vary as experience dictates.

eyes. As you collect these sensations, your are *aware* that your eyes need more light by which to read. You then gather *energy* and put some *action* in effect by making *contact* with the light, the solution to your problem. The need for light then *withdraws* to the background and you begin a new cycle.

Of course, not all cycles are this simple. However, all include the elements noted here.

FIGURE 15.2. The Resistances in the Gestalt Cycle of Experience

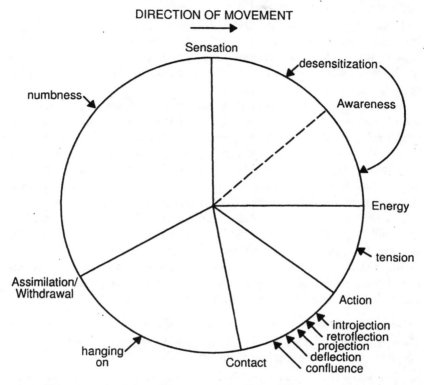

Note: The proportion of each phase to the entire cycle of experience in the diagram does not represent the actual expenditure of time or energy. These properties will vary as experience dictates.

I Know I Am Aware, But I Don't Believe I Sense Things in the Details You Mention

I hear this frequently from people. In fact, we do sense things, and then become aware. The difference is that through the course of life, we have become so accustomed to what certain sensations mean, that there is seemingly no time between the two. That is why I said that to an infant, every *sensation* is new, and gradually the infant becomes aware of the meaning of these sensations. The infant gains the ability to make rapid assessments of the meaning and actions that will resolve the awarenesses.

Let me give you an example of this development. One of my new interests is riding horses. I ride English Hunt seat, and am learning how to jump. When a horse is trotting, you post, or move up, when the horse's outside front leg moves forward. The position of the legs is called a diagonal.

When I first began to ride, I had to look down and figure out which leg was moving. I required a great deal of sensation (visual, auditory, and physical) to be aware of what I was experiencing. I then had to gain all sorts of energy to know what to do. I would make contact and move my body. The action had to be thought out step by step rather than experienced. Over time, I became able to glance down and make adjustments. Now, I instinctively know which diagonal I am posting on. If I pause, I can capture the sensations and feel the back hips of the horse move to cue me. However, it has now become automatic. I have learned to make the connection quickly.

So, take a moment in the course of your day and take in an experience more fully. Try to capture the sensations that run by so fast into awareness that they are nearly out of perception.

The cycle provides a model for change. The cycle supports the process of changing with all the resistances inherent in that process.

So, How Do I Make Use of the Cycle?

You make use of the cycle by understanding the meaning and value of each phase. Through these understandings, you will be able to encourage and guide their change process. By understanding the phase you are working in, you will more fully understand what tasks and resistances the person is facing in resolving the issue, as well as what resistances they may be working with in the moment.

NOTES

1. Gestalt Institute of Cleveland, postgraduate training program, year one.
2. Gordon Wheeler, *Gestalt reconsidered: A new approach to contact and resistance* (New York: Gestalt Institute of Cleveland Press, 1991), 88-89.

Chapter 16

The Sensation and Awareness Phase

The cycle begins with sensation: I'm sitting here and as I work, I am beginning to feel some contractions in my stomach. . . . Sensations become awareness. I am able to name and describe these sensory mechanisms.[1]

What Is the Goal of This Phase of the Cycle of Experience?

This is the first phase of the Cycle of Experience. From here, the process of change begins to become clearer. The goal is to help the person organize his or her sensations and awareness to a fuller and more conscious figure/ground. Here, there is movement from the ground of sensation to a figure of awareness. Remember, this needs time to understand and assimilate.

SENSATION AND AWARENESS

What Are Sensation and Awareness and How Do They Differ?

The phase of the Cycle of Experience called "Sensation and Awareness" is very important to understand. It is from these early experiences that the process of change begins. Sensation and awareness are different, although in our culture we tend to use them synonymously. Take a moment now to make contact with the difference as you read this material. Sensations are random sensory experiences that have no organization or focus. They bring to us no organized concept of their meaning. (See Figure 16.1.)

Awareness, on the other hand, is defined. In operation, awareness is a focused definition derived from the sensation. In awareness, our

FIGURE 16.1. The Sensation and Awareness Phase

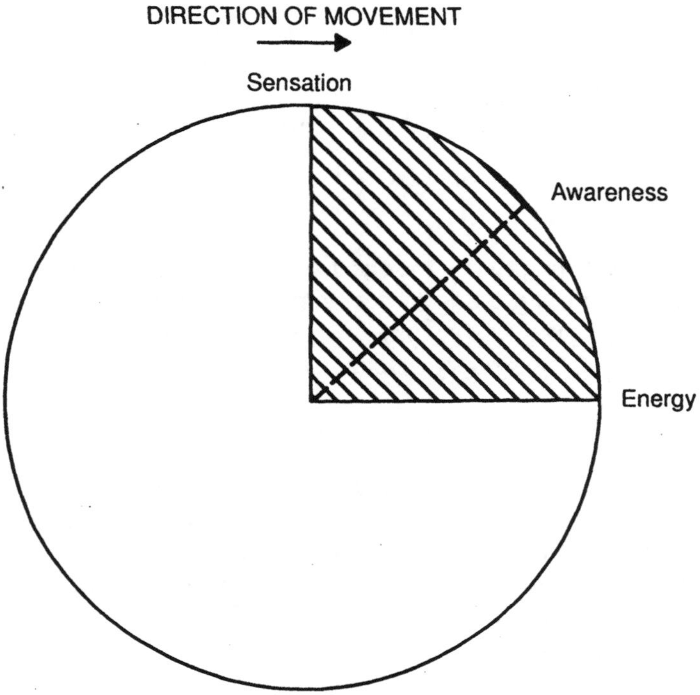

Note: The proportion of each phase to the entire cycle of experience in the diagram does not represent the actual expenditure of time or energy. These properties will vary as experience dictates.

experiences take the data from our sensations and draw a conclusion. Awareness is a recognition of what is. These awarenesses stand out and have energy. They may be feelings, wants, or desires. They possess energy, interest, clarity, and direction.

For example, think about how you first learned to read. At first, you simply sensed the contrast between light and dark on a page. Then, you became aware that these contrasting shapes were letters. Now, you have moved on one level from sensations randomness, to awareness, order.

Later, you sensed these letters and became aware that they were words. Still later, these awarenesses became the basis for still more awareness: sentences. So, you can say that awareness organizes random data and gives order to it based upon experience.

Can You Give Some More Examples of Movement from Sensation to Awareness?

An example could be seeing the numbers 2, 4, 6, 8. You would sense these numbers and perhaps have some difficulty in having any awareness of their meaning. It could be the start of the old football cheer; you know, "Two, Four, Six, Eight, who do we appreciate?" It could also mean you are numbering by even numbers, or even remembering an old locker combination.

How can you tell what you are aware of? In this case, there is not enough ground to develop the figure. Perhaps with more sensory data and the accompanying awarenesses, you would be able to differentiate the specific awareness from the many that are possible. Perhaps if you were aware of the context you would better define the awareness. Then again, you could also be aware that you are first aware of not being sure and feeling confused.

One way to learn of the difference is in your daily experience. Try an experiment. Close your eyes, then open them looking away from the direction in which you closed your eyes. What do you sense? What color do you sense? What shapes? What shadows? What smells? Now, begin to identify the objects. You have moved from sensation to awareness.

Cut a vegetable in a variety of ways: some big pieces, some slices, and some paper thin. Now, chew them one at a time and note your sensations and your awareness. Note the differences.

Why Is This Concept Important?

The concept of sensation and awareness is the building block for the change process from a gestalt viewpoint. Try shifting the focus from the simple ideas of tasting food to life. If you are unaware, or not clearly aware, of a need or desire for change, the progress toward the change will be undirected and unfocused. People become aware of their sadness about a death and decide to move ahead in life. People become aware of the stones in their shoes and choose to remove them. Men and women become aware of the anguish in a relationship and choose to work on it. People become aware of their outrage at a war and move to end it.

Sensation begins the change process. To increase our awareness of our own sensations, we move from the ground of sensation to the figure of awareness . . . . building still more ground for the next phase.

No matter what change is needed, simple or complex, important or inconsequential, you must first gain an awareness of what the "it" is.

The clearer and more defined the awareness, the easier the task of moving ahead in the change process.

During This Portion of the Cycle, Do People Always Begin with, "I Sense . . . " or "I Am Aware That . . . "?

No. In reality, people frequently come to us with an awareness in place. They might be clearly aware of a need to change a behavior or other part of their lives. Even if they come for help with a vague awareness or sensing just a discomfort in life, our goal would be the same: aid in increasing their awareness.

Is the Goal to Move from Sensation to Awareness and Then on to the Next Phase as Quickly as Possible?

No. It is best not to bound this phase, or any phase, from a perspective of time. Bound it off instead by the idea of what is needed to support the figure being developed.

Sometimes considerable time is needed in this phase to focus the awareness. People may need time to share the feelings, memories, or ideas that the awareness brings. You cannot stop when a person says, "I'm aware that I miss my father." Time may be needed to ground that figure more fully. The wider the ground, the more able the figure is to stand.

Can You Give Some Examples of This Phase of the Cycle at Work in Ministry?

The goal, the figure of your work, is to help organize sensation, or multiple awarenesses, so that work can be focused.

In a church committee meeting, the work could be rather unique. Frequently, persons enter meetings with their awarenesses in place. The task might be to move the committee backwards to collect their sensations. It could be to ask about the feelings they have as a topic is discussed: "What are you aware of as this is discussed?" In this manner, the people develop a broader figure/ground relationship and their awareness can be more clearly focused.

In the midst of a counseling session, you might do similar work. The goal of the work might be to heighten the awareness of the person's sensations, so that an awareness, a focus, can be named. Indeed, it must be named with clarity and interest in order to move ahead.

I recall working with a brave cancer patient a few years ago. At the start of our first session, she began a litany of the sensations she had. She shared that her eyes were watering, her stomach was tied in knots, and that her arms were always tight. The task was to move toward a new and clear awareness by increasing her awareness of sensations.

I was aware that she was, in essence, providing a description of herself. So, I stated the obvious, "I am curious. You have shared many sensations that you feel. I'm interested in what it is like to be you." In that statement, I provided a form around which to organize her sensations. She noted it was confusing to be her. She said, "I'm not sure who I am," and that she desired to lessen her confusion.

She then attached awareness to her sensations, "I feel like a sad, angry woman. But that's not all I want to be. I want to know who I am besides a cancer patient." She moved from random sensations of herself to an awareness of feelings and a desire to know more about herself.

This Phase of the Cycle Seems Very Similar to Figure/Ground

It is very similar. In this phase, you are indeed developing an awareness figure from the clear ground of sensations. It is important to understand the goal of the phase: movement from random sensation to focused awareness, as a movement from the ground of sensations, to the figure of awareness. You will notice that each phase of the cycle illustrates figure/ground in operation.

Some Ideas for Your Growth

As a culture, we tend to rush ourselves. We eat fast, drive fast, and talk fast. We lose the bridge between our sensations and awareness.

Take some time to slow down. Chew food; feel it as well as taste it. Look at a flower. Smell it. Are the colors even in shade, or are they varied? Take the time to sense. Be aware of how much more you might realize.

NOTE

1. Joseph Zinker, *Creative process in gestalt therapy* (New York: Vintage Books, 1978), 90.

Chapter 17

The Resistances in the Sensation and Awareness Phase

Take a moment to place yourself in the Cycle of Experience. You have sensed something, and collected an awareness. You are moving toward gaining energy to enable you to satisfy this awareness. As you would expect, there are resistances that could impede your movement toward this satisfaction.

DESENSITIZATION

What Is It, and What Value Does It Have?

Earlier in this model, resistance was viewed as a creative way of saying "No." Resistances become vehicles for the person to control the contact with another, the known and the unknown.

Desensitization is the resistance that lies between sensation and awareness. It is the resistance that allows us to moderate what we are aware of at any given moment. It is very valuable in life. Desensitization is at work every day in hospitals, as men and women work with patients. If these men and women allowed all of the sensations to become fully experienced, they would become overloaded. Desensitization is at work in our lives every day. We do not become aware of everything our body experiences. If we did, we would become overwhelmed.

I see desensitization every day in my work. At times, in the midst of a counseling session, the person appears to become highly energized. I wonder what he or she is sensing, and what the awarenesses are at the moment. I will frequently hear, "I'm not sure, Jeff. But it sure is overwhelming."

Desensitization has value in protecting us from emotional harm . . . Numbing is not always a "negative" thing . . . it can be essential.

So, How Do You "Undo" Desensitization?

First, remember there is a purpose, a place, for this resistance. If someone feels a need to step away from the stimuli, honor his/her wish, and allow it to occur. (See Figure 17.1 for a chart of this resistance.)

I tell the person the behaviors I experience. It could be the person's physical movement or a change in the person's voice. I ask an awareness question and frequently hear, "It was just a bit overwhelming." "Oh," I might say, "So, how did you feel a bit overwhelmed?" This will shift the focus back to the individual and attend to the boundary contact made apparent in the words that spoke of an "it" and not an "I."

Usually, there is some laughter here, as the person realizes he or she became an "it" for a moment. I then attend to the process, asking what the individual experienced. Then I would scale the work back a notch to a place that was a "safe emergency."

In doing this, I might ask the person to pay attention to awareness, perhaps to focus upon a smaller piece. The work then becomes more manageable for the person.

FIGURE 17.1. The Resistance in the Sensation and Awareness Phase

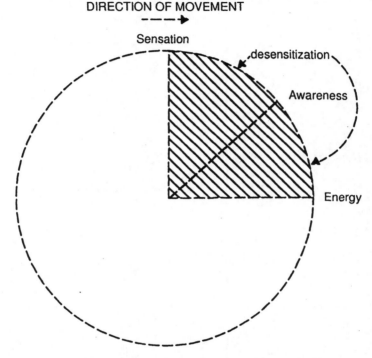

Note: The proportion of each phase to the entire cycle of experience in the diagram does not represent the actual expenditure of time or energy. These properties will vary as experience dictates.

Chapter 18

The Energy Phase

The second phase is energy/mobilization. As an awareness is defined, an individual's interest and energy begin to grow, ultimately organizing a want, a desire. Thus, competing figures recede into the background as energy is invested in a dominant content. The task of this phase is to form a sharply delineated figure out of a rich and varied ground.[1]

What Is the Energy Phase of the Cycle of Experience?

As stated so well in the quote above, the energy phase is the time of focusing within the cycle. It is during this phase that clarity is given to the figure to be worked upon. (See Figure 18.1.)

Why Is It Called the Energy Phase?
Why Not the Focusing Phase?

This phase is the result of the focusing of interest. Energy is created. I hold the analogy of the laws of physics as they pertain to a gas. A gas will encompass the shape and size of its container. If the container is large, there is no heat, no concentration of energy. If the container is small, focusing the gas, energy in the form of heat is created.

How Is This Done?

My old cross country coach used to say, "When in doubt, go back to the basics." That is true here. Keep in mind the concept of attending. The whole work of this phase is to attend to the energy you experience from the other person.

FIGURE 18.1. The Energy Phase

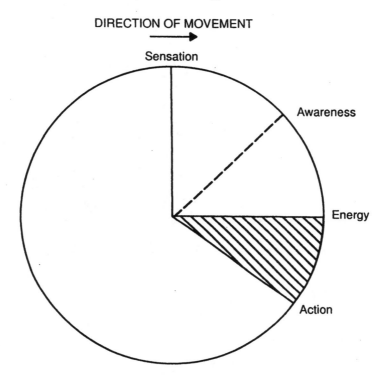

DIRECTION OF MOVEMENT

Sensation

Awareness

Energy

Action

Note: The proportion of each phase to the entire cycle of experience in the diagram does not represent the actual expenditure of time or energy. These properties will vary as experience dictates.

Can You Give Some Examples?

Pause for a moment. How do you experience or express your interest in things? Perhaps your speech quickens or slows a bit. Perhaps you begin to move or perhaps you become more still. The key is, somehow, you exhibit a change. Your interest creates a corresponding change in energy.

In this phase of the cycle, the carer tracks the changes in people's actions. The carer tracks points of energy. For example, I worked for some time with a local professional. Normally, he spoke rapidly.

At times, his speech would slow, and he would gaze around the room. I noted this to him, and he shared that he felt "drawn" into his feelings at the moment. He could no longer "surf" with his fast language and avoid contact with his own experience.

In another situation, I worked with someone who would begin to move around in his chair as certain topics were discussed. Again, I shared this observation. As with the verbal surfer, this man's contact with himself was heightened with his taking in of this simple observation.

So, You Do Not Tell Them What Their Energy Is About, Just That You Have Noted a Change?

In essence, yes. However, your task in this phase is to help focus interest and energy.

I might also note a pattern. For example, "I've noticed that each time we talk about (x) you (y)." "Each time we talk about your age, you chuckle." No interpretation is provided, just observation. This provides some ground around which to develop a figure of interest.

You then allow the people to share their meaning to what has been observed.

Energy moves us from awareness to action. Our task? To support the development of energy as part of the cycle of experience or change.

Then What Happens?

You track the level of interest, or energy, and decide, collaboratively, what they would like to work on at that moment. You might hear statements such as, "I'm feeling frightened about my job change. It's like I'm being smothered, so I run around trying to breathe." That might prompt some work concerning whether to change jobs or not, or perhaps some experiments dealing with breathing.

You might notice in a meeting that the energy drops when discussing a certain topic. This could be an interesting subject to explore. People might say, "We just feel powerless to address that topic."

So, Working in This Phase Does Not Always Mean Tracking High Energy?

Right. It means tracking the energy, or the interest people have whether that means an increase or decrease, high or low. In fact, when people find themselves losing energy, they frequently become very determined to understand the source of the energy drain.

Some Ideas for Your Growth

Attend to the energy you feel, but also beware if you do not feel energy at any given time. What are your energy signs? Do you become active or passive? Does your voice or your posture change? How do you experience your energy changes in your daily life? When your energy seems highest, do you "break contact" with people, or does your energy provide a bridge to others?

NOTE

1. Joseph Melnick and Sonia March Nevis, "Diagnosis: The Struggle for a Meaningful Paradigm." in *Gestalt therapy: Perspectives and application,* edited by Edwin Nevis (New York: The Gestalt Institute of Cleveland Press: 1992), 65.

Chapter 19

The Resistances in the Energy Phase

What Are the Resistances in This Phase of the Cycle of Experience?

There is only one resistance in the Energy phase of the cycle. This resistance impedes movement through the Energy phase, to the Action phase. (See Figure 19.1)

> In this form of blockage, a person is spinning his wheels, unable to act on his impulses. He may be mobilized, yet unable to use his energy in the service of activity which gets him what he wants.[1]

How Would I Identify This Resistance in Action?

Joseph's image of spinning wheels will help you identify this in action. Where I grew up, just west of Boston, I learned all about getting stuck in snow. It was very easy to get stuck and just spin your wheels.

We all do the same thing. Sometimes each of us will focus our energy, and not move along with it. We might be aware, or track, stomach pain, or feelings of stiffness in our limbs. These experiences and others can be signs of our resisting the movement toward action.

So, How Do I Help People Undo This Resistance?

Let us remain with the spinning wheels image. The secret to getting out of snow is very simple: all you do is press lightly on the

FIGURE 19.1. The Resistances in the Energy Phase

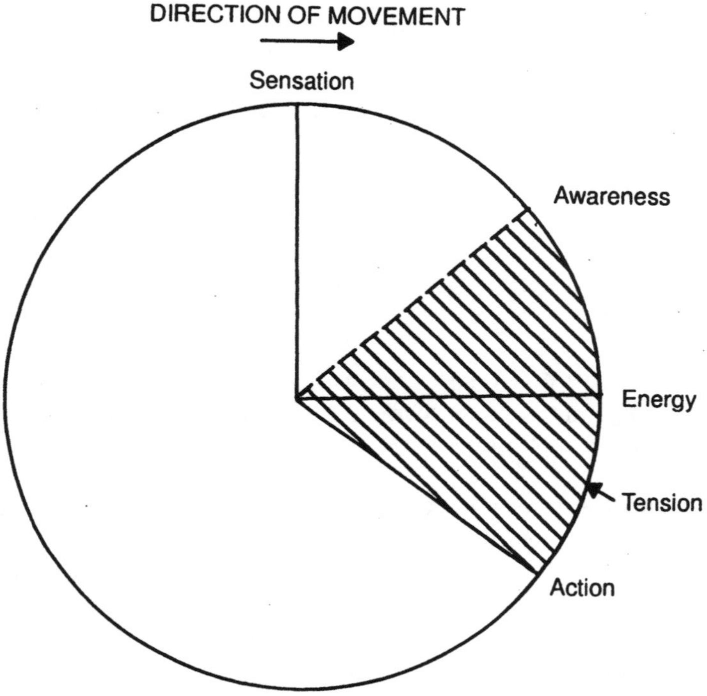

DIRECTION OF MOVEMENT

Sensation

Awareness

Energy

Tension

Action

Note: The proportion of each phase to the entire cycle of experience in the diagram does not represent the actual expenditure of time or energy. These properties will vary as experience dictates.

accelerator to allow the car to rock back and forth. Gradually, this small amount of energy moves the car out of the hole it has dug, and the car is soon on its way.

The key is to support people in releasing small, controllable bits of energy at a time. For example, individuals tense their arms as their sign of resistance. Addressing this resistance does not only mean having them shift their tension. It could mean, and indeed should begin with, drawing their attention to it, and inviting them to release it *just a bit.*

Remember, this resistance serves a purpose for people. Be careful not to just take it away.

To reduce the spinning of wheels . . . decrease energy to a manageable size . . . take away the worry and fear.

Some Ideas for Your Growth

Take a moment when you are about to do something, and hold off doing it. Instead of picking up that glass of water, tense your arm, and resist the movement toward the glass. What do you experience?

NOTE

1. Joseph Zinker, *Creative process in gestalt therapy* (New York: Vintage Press), 105.

Chapter 20

The Action Phase

You have collected some sensations and formed an awareness. Next, you have gained some energy to address this awareness. Let us say you have become aware that you are anxious about preparing a class. Somehow, you need to make contact with a way to relieve the anxiety. Perhaps you will need to vocalize the anxiety. What is certain is that you need to make contact with the anxiety in a way that is helpful. First, you have to *act*. That is where you are now in the Cycle of Experience. (See Figure 20.1)

> Here we must do something, make something change internally or agresses into the environment. In the example of hunger, we would go to the restaurant and do what was necessary to obtain the food we need.[1]

What Is the Action Phase of the Cycle of Experience?

The Action phase of the cycle is where an action, a movement, or an activity toward contact or resolution of the change needs to take place. The activity is an action that utilizes the Energy phase of the cycle to address the needs arising out of the Sensation/Awareness phase.

What Do You Mean, It Is "Activity"?

The elements of "action" occur as a vehicle to move the person, or persons, toward the point of contact—the next phase of the cycle. At the Action phase, as the energy is mobilized and moves toward contact, change begins.

FIGURE 20.1. The Action Phase

DIRECTION OF MOVEMENT

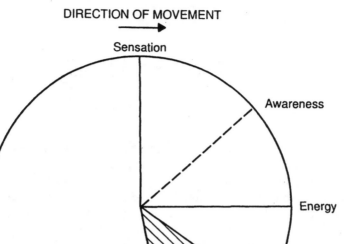

Note: The proportion of each phase to the entire cycle of experience in the diagram does not represent the actual expenditure of time or energy. These properties will vary as experience dictates.

Action ... The direct movement to satisfaction of a want or need.

At this phase of the cycle, something is begun that will eventually satisfy the need. For example, you walk to the refrigerator to get water, or you begin to speak to your family, or you begin to ask questions. In some manner, you take the energy and fuel the action toward the resolution of the want or need.

Action is the activity, whether it be " . . . movement, emotional expression; the doing."[2]

So, This Is Where the Gestalt Experiments Come Into Play?

Gestalt experiments can occur in any phase of the cycle. This is where they frequently do occur: in the Action phase of the cycle where an activity occurs in order to heighten the awareness of the need for contact so clear contact is made. Consequently, this can be a time and place where experiments might be useful. However, it is not the only place.

In several cases, I have noted that physical process was encouraged to allow contact with anger. This can be seen as one experiment. However, it is only one of a wide variety of experiments that could be done to achieve this contact. The key to the Action phase is the creativity of the facilitator to create a vehicle to move toward contact. This requires active and receptive energy, being "in the moment" with the process.

How Does Action Differ from Energy?

Energy empowers the action, the activity. Without the awareness figure, energy has no source. Without action, the energy has no transmission line to be discharged.

Some Ideas for Your Growth

How do you act? Take a few moments each day to attend to the many ways you move toward the satisfaction of your needs and desires.

Do you act quickly or slowly? Do you collect a great reserve of energy and act, or do you act only when you are ready?

When you act, do you act alone, or do you tend to enlist the energy of others? How does this relate to your own "introvert or extrovert" orientation?

NOTES

1. Margaret P. Korb, Jeffrey Gorrell, and Vernon Van De Riet, *Gestalt therapy: Practice and theory* (Needham Heights, MA: Allyn and Bacon, 1989), 24.
2. Gestalt Institute of Cleveland, postgraduate training program, year one.

Chapter 21

The Resistances in the Action Phase

Take a moment to place yourself in the Cycle of Experience. You have moved through sensation and awareness, have gained energy, and are beginning to act, to make contact and have your want/need satisfied. The resistances in this phase of the cycle are the actions that would impede the movement toward contact and satisfaction.

The first resistances are *introjects*.

What Are Introjects?

To introject something is to take it in whole, absorb it, to copy it, or to "swallow" it without reflecting upon it. The introjected element may be an idea, attitude, belief, or behavior . . . A focus in Gestalt theory may be the identification of introjects that are interfering with optimal functioning, their examination, and identification with or rejection of the introjected material.[1]

Simply put, introjects are the messages, frequently from our childhood, that define for us how we are allowed to act. These are "swallowed whole without chewing," and hence do not allow for many choices. Remember, a key element in gestalt work is aiding people to become more aware of the choices in their lives.

With introjects, people behave as if these concepts, beliefs, or ideas were in fact their own. People are no longer in contact with their choices. The choice of what to believe or how to act has, for all purposes, been taken away.

Each of us carry around introjects. Some common introjects are: "Big boys don't cry;" "Good girls are polite;" "Only weak people work for the underdog;" and "Never ask for help." If you take a few minutes, you can think of many more. These introjects dictate our responses to situations. Without choice, we simply act.

What Effect Do Introjects Have on the Cycle of Experience?

Introjects function as censors in our work toward satisfying our needs. They can create the message, "I can't change because . . . " The easiest way to understand the effect is to imagine yourself walking around the cycle.

Your trip begins at the Sensation/Awareness phase of the cycle. You have had sensations and now have a figural awareness. You desire to clarify your feelings concerning, say, sharing your feelings during sermons. Great.

You have a figure, and you are gaining energy to work with it. You begin to develop ways to satisfy this need. You are beginning to act when suddenly, you bump into the censors, the introjects. You experience them fully: "Grown men don't feel, let alone share feelings . . . If you let people know how you feel, they'll hurt you for sure . . . Boys can't feel anything except anger . . . If you try, you'll do it wrong . . . Preaching does not require feelings, it only requires facts."

Suddenly, without warning, you believe, "I can't share my feelings," though you do not know why you believe that. The introject stops your movement in the cycle by questioning your ideas, feelings, and even your right to experience.

Do Introjects Occur Only in Individuals?

No, introjects are present in all levels of systems; many are in religion. Pause for a moment and recall some "rules" you were given: "People who really believe in God are always happy. . . . If they don't believe like us, they're wrong. . . . Always pray with your eyes closed. . . . God is a man. . . . If you really believe in God, you'll never be afraid." They also exist within corporations, families, clubs, genders, races, and any other group you can imagine.

How Do Introjects Affect Our Lives?

As I said before, introjects take away or limit our choices. Introjects reduce us to reacting to situations in a nearly programmed fashion, without choice. Let me share a few examples.

While working with my local church search committee, I spoke of the options of calling either co-pastors or a female pastor to our church. My suggestion was initially met with silence and some anxious shuffling of papers. "How would a woman minister work?" a member asked. (Introject: "Ministers are always men.")

During a therapy session, I was discussing some optional ways for a young woman to speak with her father about some long-standing difficulties. In the midst of some empty chair work, I modeled, "You know, Dad, I've felt angry with you for a long time." The woman was shocked, "I could never say that. I love my father. I could never be angry at him." (Introject: "If you love, you cannot be angry, or anger means you don't love me.")

Introjects . . . well-known ideas and values of life that have become so much a part of who we are and how we act that they have been lost to our awareness.

What Harm Do Introjects Cause?

Introjects cause us to lose freshness in our living. They create stale, set styles of relating; they can also cause great anxiety.

Introjects are a framework through which we view the world. When the world changes, no longer fitting the framework we carry, anxiety occurs. To reduce the anxiety, we begin to manipulate ourselves or our environment to fit the introject. Our internal task is to maintain the integrity of the introject at all costs.

In the examples noted previously, the search committee might call the second-best applicant who is a male to maintain the introject; the woman might be polite to her father and not let him know she is angry. You or I may accept our second best because we have learned that we should not appear greedy.

How Can I Identify Introjects?

Introjects can sometimes be identified by the quickness with which people respond. Ask yourself the question, "Was the response one of choice, or one of programming?" I identify intro-jects when the statement and physical and verbal affects do not seem to be in harmony: People may share angry, friendly, or other types of words without a matching physical process. I also identify introjects when I have a hunch about where some work might lead, and encounter much resistant energy.

Do Introjects Have Any Value At All?

Yes, they do. From one level, introjects can be used in healthy manners to sustain personal morality. For example, "All men and women are equal" is an introject. "Discrimination on any grounds is wrong" is also an introject. "Obey the laws" is an introject.

Yes, introjects do have value. The task is to decide which intro-jects to keep, and which to throw away. There are also times when we choose an introject, examine it, and decide not to make it a part of our lives.

How Do You Do This?

The goal is called "undoing the introjects." When you undo introjects, people become more able to choose which beliefs are theirs, and which really belong to others.

It may not appear that difficult; however, it can be. Remember, these introjects may have been around for many generations. Keep in mind too that an introject means "I have been told to believe that . . . " So, how would you undo the introject?

If you desire to undo the image of "swallowing whole," the goal is to enable people to "chew" more fully and only take in, swallow, or believe, what they want to. The task, and sometimes the action, is to support them in saying, "I believe that . . . " Once again, you are increasing their awareness of the introject so they can choose how to relate to it.

Occasionally, I will literally ask people to preface statements with, "I believe that . . . " This is no easy task for many people, especially those who are heavily introjected. Just doing this goes against the introjects: "My ideas don't have any value" or "Don't speak unless you have something worth hearing."

I have been taught to ask them and myself to pay attention to what they experience as they speak (an introject in and of itself). Frequently, people become aware of the dissonance between what they are saying and how they feel. They have touched upon an introject. I will then spend some time exploring this figure, asking, "Now, share what you do believe, and pay attention to what you experience."

Introjects have a long, rich history in our lives, and have been usually swallowed whole by many without choice or thought. Your work is to support the person's movement toward choice: to remain with, or go against the introject. In the example of the woman who was angry at her father, there was great resistance to honoring any negative feelings about her father. We approached the introject by developing a list of feelings she could have about her father. These were developed by sharing stories about him, and being in the moment with her feelings.

Gradually, her stories shifted from the well-known and comfortable "I love my dad and he loves me," to the less comfortable and less familiar feelings. She grew to experience a variety of expressions and experiences. Gradually, she was able to gather energy, to address and define her own feelings about her father.

How Are Introjects Active in Religion and Pastoral Caring?

From one level, the very fact of religious traditions speaks to the role, power, and necessity of introjects. They aid in maintaining an expression of faith.

The rigidity, not necessarily conservatism, of some religious groups can indicate the depth of introjected meanings in their religion. These can be helpful as well as difficult. Introjects can, and perhaps need, to be addressed as persons claim their own faith. Frequently, we carry the faith of our families without thought. I wonder what would happen if we asked individuals to develop their own statement of faith as part of the religious process.

In my own life, I left my home United Church of Christ congregation in tenth grade to learn more of other faiths. I spent about one and one-half years exploring other Christian denominations. When I returned to my family's church, I returned with my own faith stance. Now, it was *my* church, as well as the church in which I was raised.

Introjects are present in all areas of church life. Committees have ways of doing work, and of meeting. Questions such as, "Why do we meet on Thursdays?" are frequently debated, even though no one knows why. The worship service lasts one hour, and sermons are no more than 15 minutes long. All are examples of introjects.

Introjects may also be present in the way pastoral carers provide care. Do we always pray at the end of a visit? Why not pray at the beginning? Do we believe we must always "talk religion" at a visit? Do we believe that we must always agree or be confluent with people in our congregations? Do we believe that we are the only people able to provide pastoral caring? There are countless introjects in the world of pastoral caring.

How Can I Learn About My Own?

Ask yourself the question: What are the introjects I carry about family, church, and society? Where and by whom were they created?

Some introjects occur on a family level. What are your family mottos regarding religion, the role of the family, or even the family's involvement in social action? Some introjects exist on an individual level. What are the five most important values you hold? If you recall the "levels of system" section of this model, you may understand the various levels at which introjects can, and indeed must, exist. There are cultural, political, and even regional introjects. Each introject exists to support the continuation of that level of system. The task for the level of system is the same as for the individual: choose to accept the introject fully or not at all.

Some Ideas for Your Growth

Introjects are an important part of our lives. On one level, they keep us safe; on another, they may prevent us from appreciating new ideas or experiences. This can be true in spirituality. Frequently, we have "preprogrammed" beliefs, or assumptions, about a biblical idea, reading, or theological point. Take a moment to become aware of your introjects and note how they affect your appreciation of Scripture.

Recall from memory the familiar "Love thy enemies" passage from the Gospel of Matthew. What are you now aware of as you reflect upon this passage? What do you feel, what are you experiencing *now*? What meaning does it hold for you in memory?

Now, read Matthew 5:38-48. After you read the passage, take a moment and center yourself. What are you experiencing? What meaning does the passage have now? Read it one more time. Now, what are you experiencing? What meaning does it have now? How do the meanings differ from before you read the passage? How do they differ from before you took the time to become aware of your introjects?

Are There Other Resistances in the Phase To Be Aware Of?

Yes, there are several. One is *retroflection*.

What Is Retroflection?

> To retroflect means literally "to turn sharply back against." When a person retroflects behavior, he does to himself what originally he did, or tried to do to another person or object. He stops directing various energies outward in attempts to manipulate and bring about changes in the environment that will satisfy his needs; instead, he redirects activity inwards and *substitutes himself in place of the environment* as the target of behavior.[2]

Retroflection is defined as turning into oneself, and doing to yourself what you would like to be done, or do, to another. Another definition is doing to ourselves what we would like someone else to do to another:

From a broader view:

> Retroflection is control of myself, any inhibiting or slowing down of my wants or impulses. It is the opposite of spontaneous or unexpected expression of wants or impulses.[3]

Retroflection can also be understood as the result of the confusion and conflict that exists between what I want to do and what I feel I am permitted to do—I am unable to move ahead, so I pull back into myself.

One way to envision retroflection is: what began as a conflict between the person and his/her environment has become a conflict within the person.

How Does It Affect the Cycle of Experience?

In the Action phase of the cycle, you move toward contact. You have energy, and move toward the point of contact and change. Suddenly, the energy and action shifts away from the point of contact, to you. The energy is held within, instead of moving along toward contact, closure, and withdrawal.

Is There Any Value or Benefit to Retroflection?

Yes, there is a benefit to retroflection. On one level, retroflection supports acting in socially responsible ways. Most of us, at one time or another, have said or thought, "I'd like to drive that guy off the road for cutting me off." We do not actually do it and instead "retroflect" the idea.

Retroflection is also helpful in the self-talk, and self-soothing that we perform. We are able to encourage ourselves and calm our frazzled nerves. Retroflection becomes a form of self-regulation.

How Is It Harmful?

Retroflection by itself is not harmful. In small doses, it can be helpful. The difficulty occurs when people, without thought or choice, retroflect. In these situations, people may calm or soothe themselves without the thought of gaining the support or calm of another. As usual in Gestalt, if the retroflection is done with awareness, the action becomes helpful and healthy.

Can You Provide Some Examples?

Imagine persons who, literally, hit themselves instead of the someone or something they want to hit. Granted, they could not actually hit the person at whom the anger is aimed. They could, however, let the person know they are angry.

Imagine persons who both introject and retroflect. Imagine they have an introject concerning their lack of self-worth, and calm themselves by rubbing their arms or hugging a teddy bear instead of developing soothing relationships.

How Can I Identify Retroflection in Action?

Retroflection is frequently visible in physical processes. People may begin to kick with their crossed legs when speaking of someone they would like to kick. They may soften their voices when they speak of being angry instead of raising their voices.

Others may grind their teeth instead of speaking out, or hit a chair instead of the actual object or person they want to hit.

Other people may show a high degree of muscle tension through their mouth, legs, and especially their arms. Each style of retroflection, usually apparent through physical process, in some ways illustrates the lack of satisfactory contact with the environment.

From another perspective, people may curl up, or nuzzle in their chairs when they desire to be nuzzled and comforted by another. Others may hum to themselves, or even sing a soothing song to comfort themselves. Used in this way, retroflections can be seen as helpful, needed substitutes.

Retroflection may also present itself as self-talk, as we guide ourselves through a difficult time. Retroflection might also occur when people do things for themselves that are truly interpersonal needs. It is one thing to be independent. Indeed, it can be healthy. However, when a person retroflects to the point that no one is allowed to help or be a part of his or her life, retroflection becomes unhealthy.

It Would Seem That People Could Develop Their Favorite Ways of Retroflecting

Yes, you are right. Each of us do have our favorite, or most familiar ways of engaging our retroflection.

As pastoral carers, we see people frequently enough, and in various settings, that we grow aware of how they present their

retroflection. We also may be aware of the effect retroflection has
had upon them.

How Are Retroflections Undone?

Retroflection can be undone by putting the "Paradoxical Theory
of Change" into practice, that is, by increasing or accenting the
retroflection. In essence, one retroflects less by learning to retroflect
more. For example, allowing a person to hit a pillow, really hit the
chair arm, or tighten his or her muscles might bring to awareness
the individual's true feelings. I might ask people to nuzzle themselves even tighter, or sink deeper into their chair. All are ways of
exaggerating people's lives in the present in order to support the
movement of change.

In essence, when retroflection is undone, what was a reproach
turns into an approach.[4]

Do People Sometimes Regret This "Undoing"?

Yes, some people do regret undoing their retroflections. When
people are retroflecting, in some manner, they are satisfied. They do
get their anger out, even if it is aimed back at themselves.

Regret may possibly arise from losing the sense of satisfaction,
as well as identifying the true feelings they may have. This loss of
well-developed and integrated coping mechanisms, such as
retroflection, can create internal chaos and a sense of insecurity in
some persons. Once again, these individuals need support as they
begin the process of developing new coping mechanisms.

---

*Retroflection . . . Doing to ourselves what we would like to do to another, or
sometimes receive from others . . . a slap, a hug, words of comfort, or words
of challenge.*

Can You Give an Example of a Retroflection
and Its Undoing?

A few years ago, I worked with a young man who had developed
retroflection into an art. His body was tense; he kicked with his

legs; his neck was tight, and he seldom turned his head. What I was most interested in was his arm. He would hit his hand, even his forearm, on the arm of the chair throughout our sessions.

Over time, I noticed that he would change his arm's impact and speed depending upon the topic. One day, as his voice calmly spoke about a long-standing difficulty with his father, he began to hit the chair harder and harder still. He appeared fully unaware of his action. Now was the time to approach the undoing of the retroflection. First, I wanted to increase his awareness of his voice and arm.

I invited him to try an experiment. I asked him to pay attention to his arm as he spoke, and whatever he did naturally, to begin to do it still harder. I placed a pillow on the arm of the chair for safety.

He began to speak and hit the chair as he had done before. Gradually, he paid attention to his action, and increased the speed and power of his arm action. At the same time, his voice became more forceful. Suddenly, he crossed his normal threshold and began to raise his voice, hitting the chair still harder.

The words he spoke were the same as before. The difference was that he was not retroflecting. Now, the energy moved out instead of in, and he was able to release the pressure he placed upon, and within, himself. He both yelled and struck out. His words were clear as he spoke of the pain and anger he had held back, displayed overtly through his hitting.

In a very different manner, I have had to aid in a person's development of retroflection. Once, I worked with a woman who wanted to "nail" her boyfriend. She was angry, and wanted to humiliate him at work. She had devised a very good plan to accomplish this.

The task was to develop a wider variety of choices of behaviors to, in essence, retroflect her original idea but not her intent.

How Might This Present in My Ministry?

Retroflection is frequently seen, as can be expected, in counseling sessions. People frequently live in fear of revealing what they truly feel. It may also be visible when someone is extremely self-caring, unable to ask for the caring of others.

Retroflection can be seen in meetings, when persons are afraid to "make waves" and keep ideas to themselves. It can also be apparent when people seem to pull their words back into their mouths and need to be encouraged to speak on.

I often notice retroflection in family counseling sessions. Frequently, children will be fearful of stating their feelings or ideas. They have introjected meanings of family, and now retroflect the expressions of their feelings. I experience this when I notice people habitually clearing their throats, or seem to begin a statement, only catch the words in their mouths.

I will support their self-expression, including their need to resist, by aiding in emotional and physical centering, as well as body awareness. I support their development of a style of making contact while feeling under control at the same time.

Some Ideas for Your Growth

Retroflections are important to all of us. As in all of Gestalt thought, it is important that we become aware of them.

Pay attention to yourself in your daily life. When you feel misunderstood, what do you do? Do you tell people how you feel, or do you grind your teeth, and, perhaps, rub your arms for comfort? When you are anxious, what do you do? Do you talk to yourself when you would like to talk to someone else? Do you rub your arms, or curl up in a chair? Do you warmly hug yourself, instead of having someone else hug you? When you are angry, do you grind your teeth instead of speaking? Do you hit a chair instead of your boss?

Pay attention to all the ways you retroflect. Then, ask yourself these questions, "Could I get this from another person, or say what I am holding back? Could I ask for some advice, instead of giving my own? Could I receive a hug instead of curling up in a chair? Could I get comfort from others, instead of giving comfort to myself?"

Another resistance is *projection*.

What Is Projection?

A projection is a trait, attitude, feeling, or bit of behavior which actually belongs to your own personality but is not experienced as such; instead, it is attributed to objects or persons in the environment as directed *toward* you by them instead of the other way around. The projector, unaware, for instance, that he is rejecting others, believes that they are rejecting him; or, unaware if his tendencies to approach others sexually, feels they make sexual approaches to him. This mechanism, like retroflection and introjection, functions to interrupt the mounting excitement of a kind and degree with which the person cannot cope.[5]

So, projection is when we place "out there" what is within ourselves. In projection, we perceive the world in our own image, although we may not even be aware of doing it. In essence, the "I" becomes the "You."

How Do Projections Differ from Introjects and Retroflections?

In introjections and retroflections, people lose touch with their environment. They are in some manner cut off from their experience of the environment.

In projections, people are very aware of themselves and the environment. The difficulty is that they cannot identify all that lies within themselves and the environment.

Projection is also different in that it is passive. People can choose to retroflect for safety's sake. They can choose to hang on to the rules of childhood. In projection, they do not have the same choice. No real good comes from projection.

In projection, people view themselves as the passive recipients of the actions of others. In fact, they are very active participants. They themselves possess the values or attributes they state and believe that others have.

How Do You Identify Projections?

When a person projects, he or she places on others the beliefs he or she may indeed hold. He or she may simply use the word "you" when speaking of an attitude or idea of someone else. In fact, these persons are speaking of themselves.

We have all heard phrases such as, "You don't like me . . . You're mean . . . You don't even care about us . . . " From a gestalt perspective, the person or persons are not sharing a belief they hold about the other persons, but rather a belief the person(s) have in themselves.

Projection . . . Putting ideas or values that are really parts of ourselves upon someone else . . . Our "I" becomes "You."

So, How Do You Undo Projections?

First, I note to the people their use of the word "you." Then I ask them to substitute the word "I" or "me" for "you." The responses become, "I don't like me . . . I'm mean . . . I don't care about us."

The goal is to help people claim their own issues as *their own.* As you might imagine, this can be a painful experience for people. Sometimes, this experience is the moment when they begin to claim their own difficulties in life and realize their participation in problems they blamed upon others.

For this reason, it is important to remember that even though projections may be easy to spot, they are not easy for people to give up. People need support as they work on this resistance and develop new self-understanding.

Some Ideas for Your Growth

When do you project? When do you project your anger onto someone else, instead of owning it as your own? When do you project your intelligence onto someone else? When do you project your feelings of inferiority onto another?

Pay attention to the "you" statements that you make, and ask yourself the question, "Could this be true about myself, and not them?"

Are There Other Resistances?

Yes, one is *deflection.*

What Is Deflection, and How Does It Affect the Cycle of Experience?

> Deflection is a maneuver for turning aside from direct contact with another person. It's a way of taking the heat off the actual contact. The heat is taken off by circumlocution, by excessive language, by laughing off what one says . . . by not looking at the person one is talking to, by abstracting rather than specific, by not getting to the point by talking *about* rather than talking *to.*[6]

Deflection is the turning away from clear contact. It is the avoidance of contact. We experience it, and even do it, every day. We deflect when we avoid eye contact, when we shift topics in conversations, and when we tell jokes. We all have a wide variety of deflection styles. We may speak abstractly *about* something, instead of clearly *to* the subject. In deflection, we push the point of discussion aside. We create, to use a *Star Trek* term, a deflector shield. Deflection can create a weak, watered-down contact with life. Contact becomes a bit, or a lot, off target. People are off just enough to not be satisfied. In this breaking of contact, contact ceases to be "I-Thou" and becomes instead "I-It."

How Do I Identify Deflection When It Occurs?

You might notice deflection when people shift their eye contact away, tell a joke, or pause. There are many styles of deflection. I notice it in myself, and hear it from others when I am unsatisfied and cannot figure out why. For some "unknown reason," I'm just a little off the mark.

When deflection occurs frequently, people may appear confused and unfocused. Eventually, any contact is difficult. I have found that the more someone is unable to account for the lack of satisfaction, the more deflection has occurred. Deflection becomes self-fueling.

Deflection . . . The shifting of attention away from the self by words, actions, or nearly any other means.

Do Deflections Have Any Purpose?

Deflection is a way to self-regulate, or manage the level or intensity of contact. People are able to self-regulate about difficult-to-handle issues and make contact in the fullest way they can.

Remember the gestalt view of resistance. Resistances do indeed have a purpose. Resistances are creative ways of saying, "No . . . not now." If deflection becomes chronic and unaware, people can feel untouched, uncared for, and misunderstood. The goal is to support people in becoming aware of themselves.

Some Ideas for Your Growth

Pay attention in your daily life to your style of deflection. Do you deflect with broken eye contact? With humor? Take the time to identify your well-developed deflection styles.

Then, ask yourself, "What am I deflecting away from? What would happen if I didn't laugh, tell a joke, or look away?"

Are There More Resistances in This Phase?

There is one, and we have already spoken about it. It is *confluence*.

As you will remember, confluence occurs when we become too much in the flow with another person or idea. We become invisible, undifferentiated from the other. As a resistance, confluence occurs when we revert to the old, known way of behaving. In essence, we become in step with what we are trying to change.

How Can I Identify Confluence in Action?

As I mentioned before, confluence can be experienced when we feel that we, or others, are agreeing too quickly, appear to put up little resistance, or share few ideas of their own.

How Can I Undo Confluence?

On one level, you can say, "You know, I'm really interested in what you have to say." I have occasionally asked people, "If you could name a solution of your own, what might it be?"

Confluence . . . Becoming one with another and losing personal iden-
tity . . . Awareness of the other and self as one.

I have found that after people begin to undo confluence and claim their own ideas, they then face another undoing challenge. For some people, being confluent, not making waves, is a well-integrated introject. The task of undoing confluence then extends beyond stating an idea; it means coming face to face with a well-integrated introject.

See Figure 21.1 for a graphic representation of the resistances in the Cycle of Experience.

FIGURE 21.1. The Resistances in the Action Phase

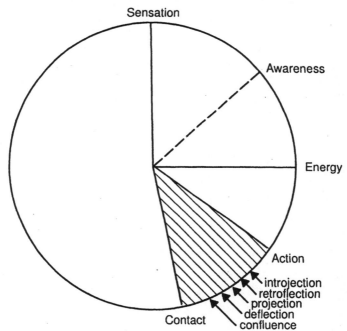

Note: The proportion of each phase to the entire cycle of experience in the diagram does not represent the actual expenditure of time or energy. These properties will vary as experience dictates.

NOTES

1. Erving Polster and Miriam Polster, *Gestalt therapy integrated: Contours of theory and practice* (New York: Vintage Books, 1973), 56, 57.

2. Frederick Perls, Ralph H. Hefferline, and Paul Goodman, *Gestalt therapy: Excitement and growth in the human personality* (Highland, NY: The Gestalt Journal Press), 1994, 391.

3. Gestalt Institute of Cleveland, postgraduate training program, year one.

4. Frederick Perls, Ralph H. Hefferline, and Paul Goodman, *Gestalt therapy: Excitement and growth in the human personality* (Highland, NY: The Gestalt Journal Press), 1994, 393.

5. Frederick Perls, Ralph H. Hefferline, and Paul Goodman, *Gestalt therapy: Excitement and growth in the human personality* (Highland, NY: The Gestalt Journal Press), 1994, 393.

6. Polster and Polster, 89.

Chapter 22

The Contact Phase

What Is "Contact"?

> Contact is not just togetherness or joining. It can only happen
> between separate beings, always requiring independence and
> always risking capture in the union. At the moment of union,
> one's fullest sense of his person is swept along into a new
> creation. I am no longer me, but me and thee make
> we. . . . Contact is the lifeblood of growth, the means for
> changing oneself and one's experience of the world. . . . So,
> contact involves not only a sense of one's self, but also the
> sense of whatever impinges at the contact boundary, and even
> merges into it. . . . Contact, however, inherently involves the
> risk of loss of identity or separateness. In this lies the adven-
> ture and the art of contact.[1]

Contact is the interaction between the person and his or her
environment in such a way that the need for change is satisfied.
Contact is the point of change. In the first section of this text, we
discussed "Contact Boundary Regulation." If you do not remember
it, it may be wise to reread it now. The point of contact is where
what is known and what is unknown meet. It is where the thirst for
water finds water, where the need for human touch finds it, where
the anger at losing a father meets some resolution of the anger.

Is This Where the "Theme" Becomes Important?

Yes. Do you remember that theme is the uppermost figure plus
direction? The clearer the uppermost figure and direction, the more
satisfying the contact.

Can You Give an Example?

Recently, I worked with a woman who was grieving over a series of "bad" relationships. There was a pattern in her life of dating "stray puppies" and then becoming angry when they left after she had "nursed them back to health."

The theme for the work was: I want to stop having relationships with unhealthy men (uppermost figure); I can go with the want, stop having these relationships, or against it, and continue to meet "stray puppies (direction)."

We worked the theme well, and she was able to move through the introjects such as "Good Christians take care of people" and the retroflections made present in her closed, frightened, sitting position.

The action was an experiment about accenting her sitting position, and her bringing her body to a more upright posture as she would describe herself and her experiences.

As her body came to just above horizontal, her voice deepened and she sounded stronger. As she continued to sit up, her voice became stronger still. Finally, she not only sat up, she stood up and said, "How do I expect to meet anything but stray pups if I act like one!"

This was the point of contact: where the known (behaving like a lost puppy) met the unknown (acting in a new, less helpless fashion). She made contact with her own projection—they are lost puppies. Together, we explored the feelings of anger, embarrassment, and fear more fully.

What Happens If I Do Not Reach Good, Clear Contact?

The system, the person or people, becomes frustrated and loses energy. That is why the work is focused around the Cycle of Experience as a model for change. Imagine that no contact is made. There is no satisfaction, no end to the need and want.

Contact . . . When the "I" meets the "Thou" . . . When "What I know" meets "What I do not know" . . . When change takes place.

What Do You Do When You Are Working in the Contact Phase and Contact Is Not Clearly Made?

I assume that one of the resistances has gotten in the way. I do a quick check of myself as to what I sense the resistance to be and move from there. I will even note that we seem to be stuck, and collaborate with the client concerning what to do next.

How Do I Apply Contact to My Ministry?

One theme I hear frequently when I work with church leaders and members is how frustrating the church work can be. Too often it seems, decisions seem to drag on far too long and people feel as if little is being accomplished. From a Gestalt view, "contact" is clearly not being made.

Another way to conceive "contact" being utilized in ministry is in keeping the Cycle of Experience in focus. Without the Contact phase, there can be no resolution of the sensation and awareness, no place of energy release, and no contact for the action taken.

Imagine a church council meeting where people note dissatisfaction about the physical condition of the sanctuary. The awareness is that too often, a small group of people decide what is needed to be done to the sanctuary.

The action could be increasing awareness of options on the part of council. Contact could come from a decision made or a committee appointed to complete the task. Contact could occur when there is a fuller participation by the council members and a decision or statement is made. Contact originating from the action, making present a variety of solutions, can have a wide variety of contact points.

As you have heard many times, taking the time to create a full figure in awareness allows the energy to be focused and a clear decision about action to be made. Then contact (or as the gestalt writers define it, satisfaction) will occur. The actual way of achieving contact is the joy of gestalt relationship and creativity.

In pastoral caring, contact occurs in the same way. People move through the cycle and feel contacted and satisfied. Couples make contact when they state their views on a difficult issue or when they share a feeling instead of a thought. Children may feel they make contact when they feel heard by their parents. The ill may feel contact has been made when they believe people have heard their desire to die.

What Is "Satisfaction" in This Context?

This term can be confusing since we usually equate "satisfied" with feeling content or happy. Although these feelings might be the result of the Contact phase, this is not always the case.

"Satisfied" in this context is similar to the word "resolved." In the Contact phase, the energy movement beginning in the Sensation/Awareness phase is resolved in the Contact phase, and the person or people experience a sense of contact and completion.

For example, a person may be working on a theme of identifying a vague awareness about a family relationship. "Satisfaction" may be the experience of identifying and expressing the feeling–which may or may not be happy.

Another person may be working on a theme of making contact with feelings about parenthood. The Contact phase may be the place where the individual feels satisfied in his or her expressions of joy and happiness.

Why Is Contact So Important?

As will be understood more fully in the next phase, if contact does not occur, people remain unsatisfied and frustrated. Supporting contact occurs allows people to move ahead to new sensations in life. Without the fullness of contact, people become stalled, unable to move ahead to new experiences.

Without contact, the children who now feel heard still would feel distant. Without contact, they still would feel isolated. Without contact, the couple continues to feel that they misunderstood each other. See Figure 22.1 for a graphic representation of the Contact phase.

FIGURE 22.1. The Contact Phase

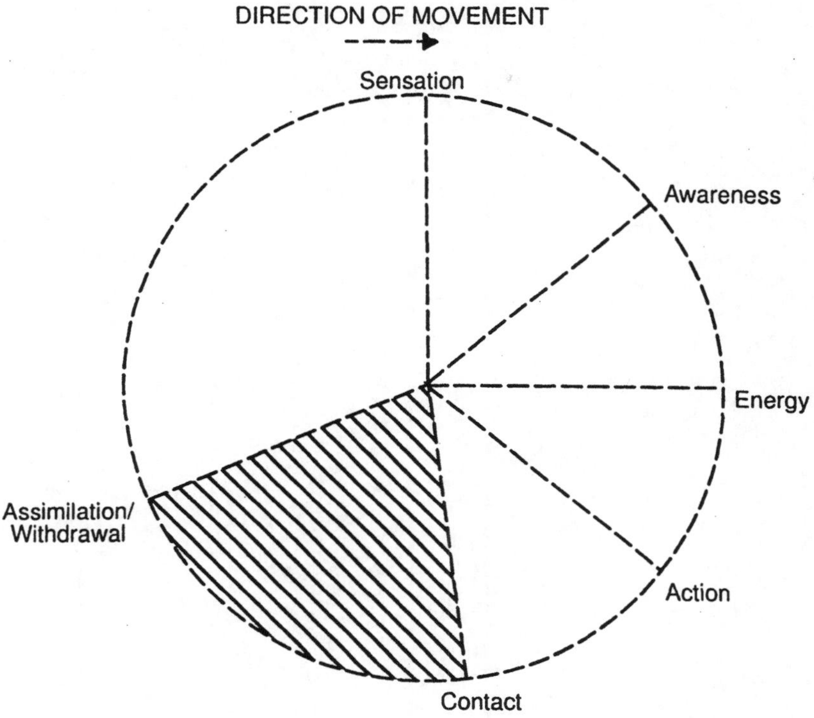

DIRECTION OF MOVEMENT

Note: The proportion of each phase to the entire cycle of experience in the diagram does not represent the actual expenditure of time or energy. These properties will vary as experience dictates.

NOTE

1. Erving Polster and Miriam Polster, *Gestalt therapy integrated: Contours of theory and practice* (New York: Vintage Books, 1982), 99, 100, 102.

Chapter 23

The Resistances in the Contact Phase

Attend to where you are in the cycle. You have made contact, and found satisfaction in the cycle. Now, you must let go and move on to new awarenesses. First, however, you must assimilate what you have learned.

So, what could occur that would resist the movement from contact, to closure, or assimilation and withdrawal? Hanging on too long.

> The individual who interrupts contact and withdrawal is not able to let go at the height or culmination of his experience. He hangs on to the experience beyond the point of optimal return and may use the defense of denial to shut out sensations of fatigue, heaviness, and dullness.[1]

People can "hang on" too long and delay the process. They can postpone the ending of the Contact phase and interrupt the movement to closure. People hang on in a variety of ways. Some might not admit that little or nothing has been learned and they need more. Others might be unable to move beyond where they are or even imagine a new experience beyond the present one. Still others might resist the integration of new ideas.

It Would Seem That Holding on Could Have a Purpose, Too

Sometimes it does. As I mentioned early in this section, the Contact phase must be attended to fully, not rushed through. Sometimes, we must intentionally hold someone to the process of closure to aid in the individual's full assimilation of the learning.

Sometimes the individual needs aid to appreciate complete and incomplete work. As mentioned before, the appreciation of closure is foreign in our culture in many respects. In order to move on to closure, we might highlight what has been accomplished. Sometimes, we need to accent it for clarity and learning. See Figure 23.1 for a graphic representation of the Contact phase of the Cycle of Experience.

FIGURE 23.1. The Resistances in the Contact Phase

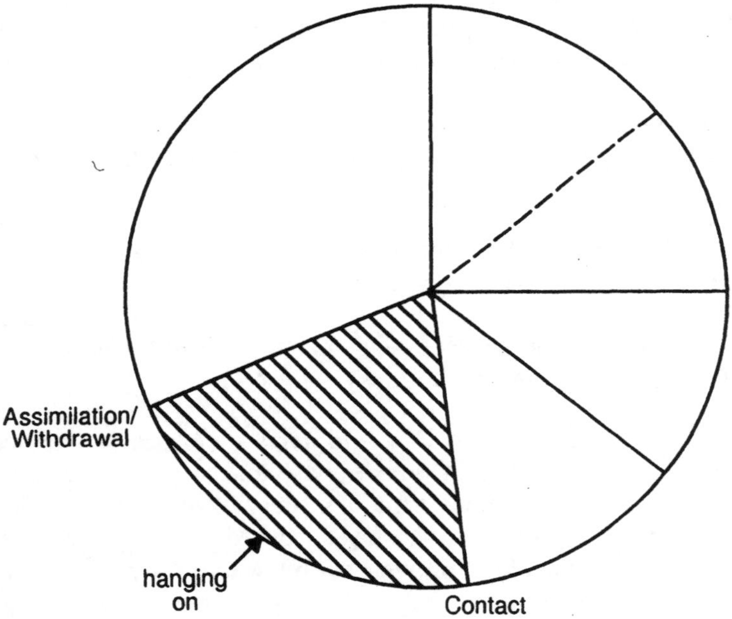

Note: The proportion of each phase to the entire cycle of experience in the diagram does not represent the actual expenditure of time or energy. These properties will vary as experience dictates.

NOTE

1. Joseph Zinker, *Creative process in gestalt therapy* (New York: Vintage Books, 1978), 110.

Chapter 24

The Assimilation and Withdrawal Phase

You have traveled nearly the entire Cycle of Experience. You have moved from sensation and awareness, on to energy, action, and contact. Now, the task is to close the work and move ahead to new sensations and awarenesses.

This is the purpose of the final phase of the Cycle of Experience.

> Most individuals have a large capacity for unfinished situations—fortunately, because in the course of living one is fated to be left with plenty of them. Nevertheless, although one can tolerate considerable unfinished experience, these uncompleted situations *do seek* completion and, when they get powerful enough, the individual is beset with preoccupation, compulsive behavior, wariness, oppressive energy, and much self-defeating activity. . . . Until closure is brought about, if these unfinished circumstances are powerful enough, the individual, no matter how successful he is in deflected directions, can never be satisfied.[1]

An important organizing principle of Gestalt learning theory is that of closure. In our perception of the world, we tend to view incomplete, visually presented information as being complete and meaningful. A circular line that is not quiet connected at each end will be viewed as a circle; typographically incomplete letters, if they retain the main elements, will still be interpreted as meaningful letters. . . . Likewise in Gestalt therapy, there is the recognition that people strive for closure in their personal relationships, even when such closure is difficult to achieve. . . . The Zeigarnik effect demonstrates that individuals seek closure; what we really want and what we are looking for in our lives are complete experiences. When they are complete, when they are whole, they can merge into the ground of life experience so that another focus can emerge.[2]

What Is the Purpose of the Assimilation and Withdrawal Phase of the Cycle of Experience?

Assimilation and withdrawal constitute the "closure" phase of the Cycle of Experience. The act of closure is a process that moves from contact with the change, to and through "taking in" the change, and moving ahead to a new cycle of experience.

Through the process of assimilation and withdrawal, the work completed becomes ground for new figures and experiences.

I Do Not Understand Why This Is So Important; It Would Seem to Happen Naturally.

In an ideal world, assimilation and withdrawal, or closure, would happen naturally. Ideally, we would pay as much attention to how things end as to how they begin. Instead, closure tends to be passed over, or at best, attended to in a cursory manner. The choice needed is to make this final phase of the cycle just as important and selective as the other phases. In other words, we must choose to attend to full-figured closure.

When Does It Happen?

Earlier in the cycle we discussed that contact occurred when the boundaries of the "known and unknown" met and merged. Withdrawal and assimilation begin when these boundaries begin to reemerge. This may be visualized as two overlapping disks that begin to separate into two distinct disks.

It is important to remember that even though we are at the end of the Cycle of Experience, contact itself does not necessary end. Contact may need to continue in order to acknowledge what is finished/unfinished, learned and unlearned, regretted/appreciated.[3]

So, the Closure Does Not Just Suddenly Happen?

Correct, it is a process—which makes sense in the world of Gestalt.

Are There Steps Within This Phase?

Yes, there are several. First, you become aware that the work is *finished*. At this point, you sense that there is nothing more to be done. The focused energy begins to dissipate, and you feel satisfied that the work is finished.

Next, there is *closure*. This is the point of acknowledgment and appreciation of what has been done, and what is left to be done—what is finished and what is unfinished.

Next, *withdrawal* occurs. It is here that there is a shift of attention away from the experience, back to a resting state where new experiences can be lived. The idea of a resting place is difficult for some to grasp. Remember the Cycle of Experience. The cycle begins at rest, moves to Sensation, and then on through the cycle. Without the place of rest and varied choices, there is not an opportunity for new awarenesses and figures to develop.

Finally, there is *assimilation*. This is not a passive state. Rather, the action of assimilation aids in the integration of the new experience and learning for future use. The learning is digested and transformed into a state that can be accessed. In the action of assimilation, the person or persons become redefined in some way by the action accomplished in the cycle.[4] See Figure 24.1 for a graphic representation of the Assimilation and Withdrawal phase of the Cycle of Experience.

I believe that the process of assimilation and withdrawal is crucial and unique in working from a Gestalt framework. It is here that the learning that has taken place is understood. Here, transformation is acknowledged as something new has been added to the person's existence. In my work, this phase of the cycle holds a feeling of sacredness as the old has become background for the new—the death of one experience and the potential birth of another.

Assimilation and withdrawal . . . The taking in of the new figure and making it part of the new ground . . . More than simple closure.

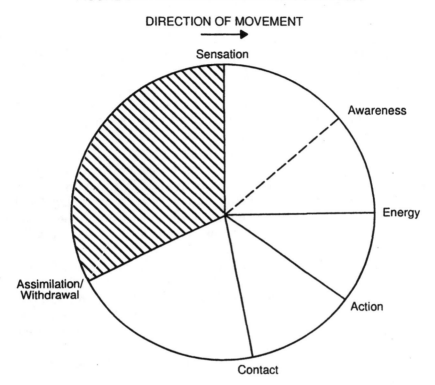

FIGURE 24.1. The Assimilation and Withdrawal Phase

Note: The proportion of each phase to the entire cycle of experience in the diagram does not represent the actual expenditure of time or energy. These properties will vary as experience dictates.

How Do You Attend to This Phase in Your Work?

First, try an experiment. Think about your closure styles for a moment. How do you close conversations? Do you close abruptly? Do you review what was said and then close? Do you get tired of the topic and just drop it?

We each have preferred styles of closure. For this reason, you must attend to the style that best suits the people and situation in which you find yourself. Attending to the needed style of closure aids in the assimilation of the experience.

For example, when I am working with people who have difficulty assimilating ideas on their own, I will close with a review of the session and ask what they are taking away with them. This provides an opportunity to verbalize ideas and share the meaning of the work in an "in the moment" fashion. I then spend some time shifting to their experience as they close. This again helps them to appreciate the change they have experienced and frees them for the next experience as well as supporting their leaving the session itself with a feeling of safety and closure.

Sometimes, I will provide some experiential feedback. I may share how *I* feel about work that was done. In this way, I allow opportunities for closure not only for the person, but for all of the members of the system. In general, I aid in helping people identify what happened in the session, what did not happen but could happen later, and what they may take away with them.

Since most of my work is with longer-term pastoral counseling, I may allow people to leave issues "hanging" for the purpose of growth. They may need to feel unfinished, and this feeling may become the figure of the next session. However, for most pastoral caring situations, clear, clean closure, withdrawal, and assimilation is preferred.

Can You Provide Some Examples?

Think of how church meetings are conducted. There are meetings that end with people feeling unsatisfied, with little accomplished. In a meeting, you might note the amount of time left, and as the time draws to a close, intentionally have people attend to what was done, as well as what was undone.

I sometimes ask people to go around the room and briefly state what they are taking from the meeting. At other times, I might share what I am taking away, and ask for others' ideas as well.

In a counseling situation, I might note the change in energy as well as the closure that I sense occurring. I might then state clearly, "I am curious about what you will be taking away with you today." In this way, I frame for them the work they have done, and provide an opportunity to affirm and bless that work.

In a worship setting, it can be important to close the service with a hymn and/or benediction that somehow speaks to the theme of the day. In this way too, the entire Cycle of Experience can be used as a model for worship movement from sensation and awareness, through contact and closure

It all situations, closure needs to be attended to and accomplished with a number of choices. Without closure, work never feels complete. Without an opportunity for assimilation, the knowledge may not be cemented well into the person's life. Without the work of this phase of the cycle, experiences live in isolation, without the opportunity of fostering future learnings and actions.

Some Ideas for Your Growth

Closure and withdrawal are important elements in full living. Without them, people cannot move ahead to new ground and figure. What are your closure styles? Do you tend to "hang on" a bit too long, or let go a bit early? Pay attention to yourself and ask the question, "Have I gained optimal learning from this experience or have I lingered too long, or left too early?"

NOTES

1. Erving Polster and Miriam Polster, *Gestalt therapy integrated: Contours of theory and practice* (New York: Vintage Books, 1982), 36-37.

2. Margaret P. Korb, Jeffrey Gorrell, and Vernon Van De Riet, *Gestalt therapy: Practice and theory* (Needham Heights, MA: Allyn and Bacon, 1989), 8-9.

3. Gestalt Institute of Cleveland, postgraduate training program, year two.

4. Gestalt Institute of Cleveland, postgraduate training program, year two.

Chapter 25

The Resistances in the Assimilation and Withdrawal Phase of the Cycle

What Could Block the Movement from Assimilation and Withdrawal to Sensation and Awareness?

Remember where you are on the cycle: You are completing the cycle, assimilating the new material, and moving ahead to new sensations and awarenesses. A resistance is an attitude or action that impedes the experience of sensations. See Figure 25.1 for a graphic representation of these resistances.

One simple way to understand it: numbness. A person may become unaware, unable to sense any type of completion, and therefore unable to collect any sensations or data of any type to provide the ground for a new Cycle of Experience.

How Do You "Undo" This?

I have found that a simple review of the work done can provide sufficient ground for a new sensation. This is not only true for those who appear to have some difficulty in moving ahead in the cycle, but for all people and situations.

To support your own appreciation of the cycle, try to review the journey you have taken to prepare for the next session, meeting, or other interaction.

Sometimes, people need to be aided in appreciating complete and incomplete work. As mentioned before, the appreciation of closure is foreign in our culture in many respects. Sometimes, we need to accent it for clarity and learning.

FIGURE 25.1. The Resistances in the Assimilation and Withdrawal Phase

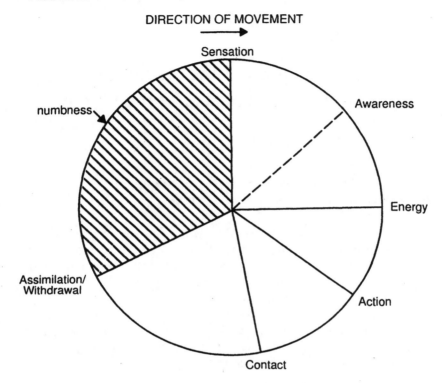

Note: The proportion of each phase to the entire cycle of experience in the diagram does not represent the actual expenditure of time or energy. These properties will vary as experience dictates.

As in all work from a gestalt perspective, an appreciation on your part of the value of this resistance is important. Ask yourself, "What might happen if they were to move ahead to a new Cycle of Experience? What are they saying 'no' to right now? What are they afraid of saying 'yes' to right now? How can I support this work in becoming a 'safe emergency' for them?"

Chapter 26

Review and Case Presentations

What Should I Be Aware of as I Apply Gestalt Principles
to My Daily Ministry?

Think back to the Cycle of Experience. Remember that if there
were no interruptions to the cycle, it would flow on its own—from
Sensation and Awareness right on to Assimilation and Withdrawal.
The problem is that there are resistances along the way which do
not permit this flow to occur.

As you are working with Gestalt principles, you must concen-
trate on answering two questions:

1. Where am I in the Cycle of Experience?
2. What resistances am I experiencing?

How Do I Answer These Questions?

These questions can be answered by trusting your experience.

SENSATION AND AWARENESS

This phase can be identified by the movement from sensation to
awareness. In this phase, people begin to state their awarenesses of
where they are and what they are experiencing in the here and now.
The present experience is paramount. Your task is to make figural
the movement from sensation to awareness. Then, support the figure development for the work of the period out of their awareness.
If they seem unable to do this, perhaps they are experiencing sen-

sory overload. Help them to clarify their sensations, so that a more complete awareness can be experienced.

ENERGY

Remember, energy is experienced through the senses. During this phase, energy is collected and the work becomes more focused. You are tracking the changes in energy made apparent through their bodies, their voices, and other perceptions you have.

One way to support the cycle in general and this phase in particular is to mirror their actions. When their energy moves them physically forward, sit forward along with them. When people cross their arms in the midst of the work, cross yours as well. Do not express these actions in an immediate fashion. That can be abrupt and shift the focus from their work to your activity. Instead, slowly parallel their actions and movements.

At the same time, attend to their changes in energy. Share your awareness of voice, body, or language changes. Of course, do not overdo it. Be selective to support the *process* of the work, not the content. Your task is to heighten awareness of energy so that they do not simply spin their wheels in this phase.

If people do seem to be spinning wheels, call attention to their pattern, "I noticed that when you began to . . . your voice dropped." I believe people spin their wheels when they are not sure about the outcome of their next step. Support the work by scaling it back a bit so they can move ahead more easily.

ACTION

The Action phase can be identified by the doing of something. In this phase, people have identified their awareness, gathered energy, and now are doing something to make contact.

In this phase, there are many resistances. Attend to these resistances in simple ways, as stated in the Cycle of Experience portion of this project. In all of the resistances within this phase, and in all phases, be curious about the value the resistances have and the role the resistances play in the person's life. Remember, resistances are creative ways of saying "No," and need to be valued.

CONTACT

This phase can be sometimes identified by the surprise people may experience at the newness of the experience. It is in this phase of the cycle that the need/want is satisfied. Frequently, contact is experienced by an energy drop and a feeling of being at a new emotional place.

This is also where the known and the unknown come into contact. Without the support of clear contact, the participants will be unable to support or assimilate any changes. As they move toward making contact with this new part of themselves, scale back the work so that clear and not overwhelming contact can be made. Remain with the contact long enough to provide clarity of new awareness, but not so long that the contact becomes dulled.

ASSIMILATION AND WITHDRAWAL

This phase is noted by the ending of the cycle and the integrating of new awareness. It can be identified by a reflective, "How do I take this with me?" feeling. As in the Contact phase, support the participants' understanding of where they were and where they are. Support and celebrate the newness.

So Gestalt Work Happens on Two Levels: The "Big" Picture and Helping Undo the Blockages to Achieving This "Big" Picture, Right?

Yes. You are aware of the two levels on the Cycle of Experience.

On one level, people are moving around the cycle, just as the earth moves around the sun. This is a *macro* level cycle. At the same time, the earth revolves on its own axis as it orbits the sun. This orbit is a *micro* level cycle. In other words, as you are working your way around the cycle in a macro manner, you also must deal with resistances and phases in a micro way.

Years ago, I worked with a young woman who wanted to increase her ability to make her opinions and decisions known to her parents. Simply, she shut herself off when they asked for her opinion.

On a macro level, we were moving from her known, shut down side, to her unknown, more "out there" side. She was moving from an awareness of her voice becoming strained and childlike, toward her desire to become "more adult"–the macro cycle.

At the same time, we had to work on a micro level. In this case, we had to work with nearly every resistance that resided in the cycle. At the point of "spinning her wheels" in the Energy phase, we had to move from her dropping her voice as she collected energy, to keeping her voice strong. We worked a micro cycle dealing with her projections, as well as her deeply held retroflective style.

So, the Work We Might Do May Simply Concern an Introject?

Yes, it could. The work could focus upon any element in the cycle, phase, or resistance that becomes figural for the work. I have found that sometimes the most satisfying work can be focused upon increasing the awareness of and undoing of resistances.

You Seem to Ask Very Few Questions of People. Is There a Reason for This?

Yes, there is a reason. Questions can be experienced as interrogative by people. Questions tend to focus upon content, creating a duality: "I ask the questions and you answer them."

By making statements, noting your interest, curiosity, or awareness, you can keep open the relationship of mutual exploration that is central to Gestalt work.

It is rather easy to shift from a question-and-answer method of work to sharing your awareness and curiosity. Take some time and experiment with the idea. For example, if someone is speaking about his or her family, and you believe it would be helpful to hear more about the brother, you could say, "I'm curious about your brother. Tell me some more about him" or as I prefer, simply, "I'm curious about your brother."

CASE STUDIES

It can be difficult to present cases. There are so many incidents that cannot be fully shared in the printed word. The experience is just too limiting in type. So, I will attempt to share three cases that illustrate the principles of Gestalt in action.

Individual Work: Lynn

In this case, I will present the development of theme: uppermost figure plus direction, and the development and utilization of a metaphor. This case focuses upon my work with a 35-year-old divorced white female named Lynn. She has seen me for 45 sessions over a two-year period. A key theme during her therapy has been her difficulty in forming relationships with "healthy men"–she says "I usually bring stray puppies home."

The theme of the session was her anxiety concerning these relationships and her need to make a clear break from old relationships that have remained as friendships.

The Theme

Uppermost Figure: To make clean break with old relationships or not.

Direction: Chose to explore the meaning and feelings surrounding the ending of old relationships.

Sensation and Awareness

Her awareness was intense anxiety. She noted she felt anxious, " . . . as if I was about to jump off a diving board." The sensations attributed to this awareness were located primarily in her chest. She noted she felt a heaviness and a tension there. She exhibited much energy and interest in her "diving board" metaphor. So, we decided to use it throughout the session.

Energy

Her energy was located primarily in her voice and body posture. Her voice appeared strained at times, and she noted she felt "choked." As she would speak about ending these former relationships, her energy would rise and fall. She would begin with some excitement about "making a clean dive" and then feel less energy as she felt "sad, like [she] missed the dive." Together, we developed the image of "making ready for the dive." We explored what steps a diver would have to take to "make ready" for "the dive of a lifetime."

Action

The action was an experiment focusing upon taking the voice of the coach of this diver. The coach was to offer support and encouragement to this diver as she approached the dive. Together, the diver and coach would "walk through" the dive, step by step. The goal of this action was to make contact with the "brave, confident diver" side of her. My goal was to increase her awareness of her capacity for self-support in difficult times. She worked through two main resistances in the action phase of the cycle: introject and deflection.

The introject was that of her family message that she " . . . would never love a good man." This introject came to her awareness as she would critique her dive with, "I can't do this. I'll never be able to make this dive." Her deflection was through humor, as she lost contact between her role as coach and diver.

My reading of these two resistances was that we were moving a bit too fast in the session, and she was pacing herself to support her making clear contact when she was ready.

The experiment was explained: "Lynn, I'm interested in this metaphor of the diver. I'm wondering if you would like to spend some time with the dive, and perhaps find some support for yourself. (She noted she was interested.)

"Most athletes who are about to make the dive of a lifetime have a coach right there by them. They prepare together. They support each other and sometimes even fight. I've been at a few diving competitions, and one thing that has struck me was the teamwork between these two people. I would like you to take the voice of both the coach and the diver. I would like you to try to speak as the coach to the diver, and as the diver to the coach."

She shared she was interested in the experiment and got herself situated in her chair. In the course of the experiment, she presented much energy from both roles. The diver spoke of her fear and needing to be reassured that she could make the dive. The diver even asked the coach to walk her through the dive itself. Lynn did not seem anxious, just energized. She was able to provide great detail concerning "centering herself" to dive, and a large number of steps to execute the dive itself. Much of my work was to keep her in role and offer some encouragement.

As the experiment continued, the diver began to resist and doubt the words of the coach. She noted that the coach had never dove, and would not know what she was going through or what it would be like. I worked to support this conflict, viewing it as a Contact Boundary issue. I supported this by offering some words to support this known part of her, "I cannot make the dive and will talk myself out of it," and the unknown side, "I can make the dive."

This was the point of contact.

Contact

The contact occurred as the diver became increasingly angry and finally yelled, "Don't you understand? This is the dive I've been waiting for all my life, and I'm afraid! I don't want you to tell me how to make the dive. I know what to do. I want to know that you will still be here even if I fail. I am afraid I can't ever do it."

At that point, her energy dropped, and I took on the voice of the coach apologizing for not hearing and respecting her fears. She took the voice of the coach back and said, "I didn't know you were this afraid. I never knew how important this dive was for you. You're right. I do tell you what to do. I don't listen well."

As the contact continued to strengthen, she moved out of character, beginning to talk about her need to do this at her pace. She explored more fully the introject of her family, that she would never be able to make this relationship work. She became aware of the power of this introject and her need for comfort from it.

Assimilation and Withdrawal

This phase occurred with the trust that she would know when she was ready to dive. She took in her need to nurture her self-awareness and her need to pace her deepening relationships. She also affirmed the importance of this relationship to herself. This new awareness led to more exploration of her family introjects, and the "undoing" of them that occurred within this relationship.

SUMMARY

This case illustrates several key points in work from a Gestalt perspective:

1. Allow time for figure/ground to be developed.
2. Use metaphors when possible. Make sure they fit. It is best when they come from the other person, not yourself. However, there are times when your placing a metaphor "out there" can support the work, as well as be a representation of your being with the process.
3. Support the work. As this woman approached her known and unknown—the person who would keep old relationships and the person who wanted to invest fully in the existing one—there was a need for support and care.
4. Experiments, and any directed behaviors, are always collaborative in nature. They need to be developed from the material in the moment, with a foundation based in the relationship between the people.

COUPLE WORK

The second case study focuses upon work between two people. It illustrates the development of a common theme and codeveloped and performed experiments. Couple work can be any constellation of people: married, singles, siblings, parents, or children.

This case focuses upon a marriage of four years. Each person is 28 years old and they have a two-year-old son. Their therapy road has been difficult for each and both together. Therapy began during a crisis situation, and the husband has had difficulty shifting from his model of "you're (his wife) the problem here."

They tend to become polarized, projecting onto each other. When this occurs, each complains of not being listened to, and the session grinds to a halt.

Theme

Uppermost figure: A desire to increase self-disclosure statements to and from each person, or to *not* increase self-disclosure.

Direction: Chose to go with both sides of uppermost figure; express more "I" statements, as well as "you" statements.

Figure/Ground

The figure was the projective style of each within the sessions. In effect, the figure was one of their resistances. The ground for this was the awareness of the small number of "I" statements made in session, and the great number of "you" statements. The figure was an "aha" experience after a few minutes of attending to their words. Each was unaware of their pattern.

Sensation and Awareness

Each noted anxiety in the chest as the work progressed. Each noted feeling "anxious and afraid" of being more fully known by the other.

Energy

The energy was made apparent through their voices and the "angry tone" each had as work progressed. The anger seemed most apparent when the projections increased. Both the person projecting and the person responding to the projection became increasingly angry.

Action

The action was a simple experiment accenting their well-developed projections. They were to make statements in pairs: one statement as a projection, "You . . . " and the next as an "I" statement. They were asked to track what they experienced both as the "transmitter and receiver" of these messages.

As each gave feedback about how they perceived themselves and each other, the pace of the work slowed. The "I" statements became increasingly self-revealing, and the "you" statements became less powerful. This increasing self-revelation occurred as a natural consequence of the experiment, rather than one forced by the participants. As the experiment continued, their voices became softer, and their affect more connective with open body posture and more leaning toward each other.

Contact

The contact occurred when after seven or eight pairs of statements exchanged, they both stopped. When I asked them to report what they were experiencing, each said they felt increasingly uncomfortable projecting onto the other and more comfortable revealing their ideas and feelings. This was a surprise to each. Both noted they enjoyed experiencing the other more fully.

When I then asked them to continue with the experiment, they became angry at me and protective of each other. They protested, stating they wanted to work on the "I" statements more, feeling that I was "accenting the past" when I encouraged them to continue with the whole experiment.

Assimilation and Withdrawal

The Assimilation and Withdrawal phase continued from the Contact phase as they attended to their feelings concerning projecting versus self-disclosing. They spoke to each other, naming the feelings they had in the moment. I encouraged them to share the meaning the session had for them, and make one statement regarding what they hoped to take with them from the session. Each stated they hoped to continue self-disclosure at home and focus upon it in their work with me.

SUMMARY

In this work, my desire was that the couple would learn more of their desired behavior by accenting the one they exhibited. I utilized the Paradoxical Theory of Change in a modified fashion.

By attending to the nondesired behavior, which they seemed to do naturally, they became more aware of their options. They became more aware of the process of self-revelation as they accented projection. In this case, had they not had the opportunity to experience the "sting" of projection, they may not have been able to appreciate and assimilate the value of self-disclosure. This case also illustrates the power and value of having persons talk to each other and not through the counselor, as so easily can occur when working with couples or families.

GROUP WORK

This case does not focus upon conducting group therapy. Rather, it focuses upon the utilization of the Cycle of Experience, as it might be applied to group process. This could include church meetings, committee meetings, or any gathering of people.

This case focuses upon a committee of five people. They have met three times to discuss the mission program of a local church. In this committee, one person (frequently the same person) directs the work and opinions of the group. Essentially, whatever direction the meeting begins with is the direction which will continue until the meeting ends. The meetings contain one issue and one topic.

My goal was simple: Increase the level of group participation.

Figure/Ground

I followed the process of the group for several minutes. I attended to the people who spoke and those who did not speak. I noted that the longer the time spent with one person dominating the time, the less interaction occurred. In essence, the longer one person spoke, the less likely it was for other persons to join in the meeting.

Theme

Uppermost figure: More people verbally participating in meeting (need/want); keep number of persons participating low (resistance to the need/want). I wondered if this was an introject from former leadership or an unaware group rule.

Direction: Go with the desired change and have more people speak; go with the resistance and have fewer people speak; or alternate between the two poles. The decision was made to go with the "more people speak" direction of work.

The actual work of this theme was done in the second half of the 90-minute meeting time.

Sensation and Awareness

I asked each person to share where he or she was as the second half of the meeting began. Each was aware of feelings of anxiety concerning the desire and potential of changing the pattern of the meeting.

Energy

The energy was apparent through laughter and through silence as the meeting continued. Laughter would occur as a seldom-heard person spoke, as well as when a previously "head spokesperson" was more silent than usual.

Action

Here is the trick in this session: the action was the simple act of reporting what they were experiencing. In this action, all voices were heard, and each person was able to be "in the room" at the same time.

Contact

The contact occurred as I noted to them my awareness of hearing some voices for the first time. Spontaneously, *each person* shared how it felt to hear every person. They shared feelings of welcome, excitement, and relaxation in hearing the many voices and feeling the connection with all members of the group.

Assimilation and Withdrawal

I asked participants to go around the room again, sharing in a few words their awareness in the *now.* Each person spoke of wanting more "community" at these meetings, and less of the "vocal minority and silent majority." We ended the phase by promising to all report in at the start of each meeting.

SUMMARY

I presented this case to demonstrate that gestalt work does not have to be complex or daring. It can be as simple as getting people to talk.

In this case, I wanted to demonstrate the value of somehow getting each person involved in the meeting from the start. I have found that then, if a person chooses to remain silent for the remainder of the meeting, he or she is still experienced as being part of the community.

I also wanted to demonstrate the value of the here and now work of Gestalt. At no time did people talk about how it "used to be," feeling distant, separate, and disconnected. Instead, they spoke about how it was, then and there, to, with, and beside each other working as a covenant team.

Bibliography

Achtemeier, Paul J. *Proclamation commentaries: Mark.* Philadelphia: Fortress, 1975.

Boisen, Anton. *The exploration of the inner world.* Lanham, MD: University Press of America Inc., 1936.

Bultman, Rudolf. *The Gospel of John: A commentary.* Philadelphia: The Westminster Press, 1971.

Capps, Donald. *Pastoral care: A thematic approach.* Philadelphia: The Westminster Press. 1979.

Childs, Brian H. *Short-term pastoral counseling.* Nashville: Abingdon, 1990.

Corsini, Raymond J., Editor. *Current psychotherapies.* Itasca, IL: F.E. Peacock Publishers, 1984.

Dayringer, Richard. *The heart of pastoral counseling: Healing through relationship.* Grand Rapids, MI: Zondervan Publishing, 1988.

Firet, Jacob. *The dynamics of pastoring.* Grand Rapids, MI: William B. Erdmans Publishing Company, 1983.

Fuller, Reginold. *Studies in theology: A critical introduction to the new testament.* Letchworth, Hertfordshire, England: Duckworth, 1971.

Gagnon, John H. "Integrated field theory in eclectic psychology: The metamorphosing gestalt." *The Journal of Pastoral Counseling* 19 (Spring-Summer 1984).

Graham, Larry K. *Care of people, care of worlds: A psychosystems approach to pastoral care and counseling.* Nashville: Abingdon, 1992.

Hatcher, Chris and Himelstein, Philip, Editors. *The handbook of gestalt therapy.* New York: Jason Aronson, Inc., 1976.

Jackson, Gordon E. *Pastoral care and process theology.* Lanham, MD: University Press of America Inc., 1981.

Knights, Ward A. "On being a CPE supervisor." *Journal of Supervision and Training in Ministry* 1 (1978).

Korb, Margaret P., Gorrell, Jeffrey, and Van De Riet, Vernin. *Gestalt therapy: Practice and theory.* Needham Heights, MA: Allyn and Bacon, 1989.

Latner, Joel. *The gestalt therapy book.* Highland, New York: The Gestalt Journal Press, 1973.

Maslow, Albert R. "Freedom from 'the known' in psychotherapy." *The Journal of Pastoral Counseling* 22:2 (1987).

Naranjo, Claudio. *The techniques of gestalt therapy.* Highland, New York: The Gestalt Journal Press, 1980.

Nevis, Edwin C., Editor. *Gestalt therapy: Perspectives and applications.* New York: The Gestalt Institute Press, 1992.

Oden, Thomas C. *Pastoral theology: Essentials in ministry.* San Francisco: Harper and Row, 1985.

Ogelsby, William B. *Biblical themes for pastoral care.* Nashville: Abingdon, 1987.

Perls, Fritz. *Ego, hunger, and aggression.* New York: Vintage Books, 1947.

Perls, Fritz. *The gestalt approach and eyewitness to therapy.* New York: Science and Behavior Books, 1973.

Perls, Frederick. *Gestalt therapy verbatim.* New York: The Gestalt Institute Press, 1988.

Perls, Frederick, Hefferline, Ralph F., and Goodman, Paul. *Gestalt therapy: Excitement and growth in the human personality.* London: Souvenir Press, 1951.

Polster, Erving and Polster, Miriam. *Gestalt therapy integrated: Contours of theory and practice.* New York: Vintage Books, 1982.

Renear, Miles. "Therapy and theology: The continuing dialogue." *The Journal of Pastoral Care* 30 (March 1976).

Ryan, Barrie. "The lost self-changes: Gestalt and christian concepts of rebirth." *Journal of Religion and Health* 15 (October 1976).

Scharff, Jill and Scharff, David. *Scharff notes: A primer of object relations therapy.* Northvale, NJ: Jason Aronson Inc., 1992.

Stevens, John O. *Gestalt is.* Moab, Utah: Real People Press, 1975.

Swanson, J. (1988). Boundary process and boundary states: A proposed revision of the gestalt theory of boundary disturbance. *The Gestalt Journal, (8)*1, 65-71.

Wendel, Virginia S. "Counseling: A conversion experience." *Pastoral Psychology* 38 (Fall 1989).

Wheeler, Gordon. *Gestalt reconsidered: A new approach to contact and resistance.* New York: The Gestalt Institute of Cleveland Press, 1991.

Wise, Carroll A. *Pastoral psychotherapy.* New York: Jason Aronson Inc., 1982.

Zinker, Joseph. *Creative process in Gestalt therapy.* New York: Vintage Books, 1977.

Index